ADVANCE PRAISE FOR THE BOOK

'Many lawyers have adorned and embellished the Hall of Legal Fame . . . The book, however, traces and maps the lives and achievements of seven of them, so that readers would feel them soar . . . achieving the unattainable. The book boasts an inspiring and thought-provoking narrative. The collection of life experiences takes one through their strengths and sensitivities, subtly hints at their flaws, and captures the significant movements in the legal profession. It makes for a very interesting read.'

ARUN JAITLEY, MINISTER OF FINANCE

'The leading lights of the law are the torchbearers of the future in which the law is supreme and makes us all accountable. The journey is not easy, but the icons in the book will play an epochal role in clearing the debris. *Legal Eagles* captures the levels of excellence that each of the torchbearers in this book have achieved. These pathfinders have done yeoman service not only to the legal profession but also to society. This book vividly brings to the reader the life and times of these great achievers.'

KAPIL SIBAL, SENIOR LAWYER AND FORMER TELECOM AND LAW MINISTER

'The legal profession is no less glamorous than that of film stars. From time to time, it throws up stars and also some superstars. The stories of some of these stars and superstars chosen by Indu Bhan for her book provide as fascinating a reading as would a book on Dilip Kumar, Rajesh Khanna and Amitabh Bachchan. Their exploits, which earned them their fame, and also their shortcomings, if any, both have been beautifully covered in this excellent book. *Legal Eagles* is surely a must-read for all lawyers and also perhaps some discerning film stars.'

SHANTI BHUSHAN, CONSTITUTIONAL LAW EXPERT AND FORMER LAW MINISTER

'*Legal Eagles* will inspire young lawyers in their future careers.'

ANIL B. DIVAN, CONSTITUTIONAL LAW EXPERT AND SENIOR LAWYER

'It makes for fascinating reading. Every member of the legal fraternity knows the legal eagles covered in the book, but not many know the interesting background of each one of them, how they started and rose by leaps and bounds, and how they have become role models for the younger generation of lawyers and law students. The book is impressive and inspiring. It is opportune as it comes at a time when the luminous stars are shining bright.'

P.P. RAO, CONSTITUTIONAL LAW EXPERT AND SENIOR LAWYER

LEGAL
EAGLES

LEGAL
EAGLES

STORIES OF THE TOP SEVEN INDIAN LAWYERS

INDU BHAN

RANDOM HOUSE INDIA

Published by Random House India in 2015
1

Copyright © Indu Bhan 2015
Foreword copyright © R.M. Lodha 2015

Random House Publishers India Pvt. Ltd
7th Floor, Infinity Tower C, DLF Cyber City
Gurgaon – 122002
Haryana

Random House Group Limited
20 Vauxhall Bridge Road
London SW1V 2SA
United Kingdom

978-81-8400-635-3

Typeset in Adobe Garamond by Manipal Digital Systems, Manipal

Printed and bound in India by Replika Press Private Limited

A PENGUIN RANDOM HOUSE COMPANY

To my loving daughter, Mahika

There is a tide in the affairs of men,
Which taken at the flood, leads on to fortune.
Omitted, all the voyage of their life
is bound in shallows and in miseries.
On such a full sea are we now afloat.
And we must take the current when it serves,
or lose our ventures.

—William Shakespeare, *Julius Caesar*, Act IV, Scene III, 218–24

CONTENTS

ACKNOWLEDGEMENTS

In my first attempt at writing a book, I never walked alone. I am thankful to all those who helped me in putting together the life sketches of the legal luminaries in this book.

My daughter, Mahika, my husband, Atul Khorana, and my niece, Nishika Bhan, all stood by me. All of them contributed indirectly in their own unique way. I will always remember their unwavering patience and persistence.

I am also indebted to those who helped me in the production of the book—C. Sasidharan, who transcribed a part of the recordings, and my other journalist friends for their valuable suggestions.

I would also like to extend my sincere and special thanks to eminent jurists Fali Nariman and Shanti Bhushan as well as senior advocate Jayant Bhushan for all their advice and guidance. I also wish to acknowledge lawyers Raian Karanjawala, Anip Sachthey and Manali Singhal for giving insights into the lives of the persons profiled in the book. I would also like to acknowledge and appreciate the cooperation of the staff of these eminent lawyers, especially Rishi Kumar, M. Thangathurai, Vinod Kumar, Anand and Narayan, and their family members as well, particularly Mukul Rohatgi's sister, Madhulika, and Justice Rohinton Nariman's mother, Bapsi Nariman, and his daughter Nina.

My thanks are also due to my friends whom I spoke with during the times I was getting restless and when tough situations cropped up.

In the end, I especially wish to thank Sunil Jain, managing editor of the *Financial Express*, for his encouragement and support.

FOREWORD

Among those who choose the profession of the law, there are some who receive the glittering prizes that success at the Bar enables. The course of a journey for them is as challenging as it is for others. *Legal Eagles* is a piece of work on seven leading lawyers of the Supreme Court of India—one of them is now adorning the bench. How did they distinguish themselves from others in the legal profession? What has gone into making them such successful lawyers? How did their families and friends help them in overcoming the many hardships and brought about an evolution in their personalities? What has been their contribution to the development of law and constitutional principles? Indu Bhan, an accredited journalist, who covers the Supreme Court for the *Financial Express*, has addressed the above and many more aspects. Only a reporter who has done extensive research on the performance of these lawyers and watched their persona could have given such an incredible account!

I first entered the Supreme Court as a spectator in 1969—it was not as difficult then to enter the majestic premises as it is now. On completion of my graduation I intended to study the law. In the First Court, a Constitution Bench of nine judges was hearing the *R.C. Cooper* case (known as the *Bank Nationalization* case). The eloquence of the two top lawyers—N.A. Palkhivala and Niren De—was the most impressive element of the show. A couple of decades later, when I became a judge of the Rajasthan High Court and later its Chief Justice, and then moved on to become a judge of the Supreme Court of India and, ultimately, the Chief Justice of India, I got the opportunity to hear all sorts of lawyers. The client-centric approach of contemporary lawyers has blurred the boundary between law and other disciplines. The impact of the continuing globalization of business, finance and commerce has brought into focus the need for courageous lawyers with the highest ethical standards. I hold the view, as many do, that the responsibility of the legal profession towards the public at large is even greater now.

In a democratic country like India, where the rule of law is the driving force in all spheres of governance, an independent and effective Bar is indispensable. The effectiveness of justice delivery is qualitatively dependent on the performance of the lawyers. Everything that goes on in the Supreme Court is related to something important and, as a part of process, it is the quality of lawyers, their knowledge, analytical skills and ability to develop legal and constitutional principles that enable the court to consistently arrive at 'correct decisions'. The judgement skills of the judges are definitely a critical factor, but the availability of quality legal assistance is directly and intimately connected to the adjudicatory process. Many important judgements delivered by our Supreme Court bears testimony to the great assistance rendered by these senior lawyers.

It is seen that when the disposal of natural resources is exposed to the ill usage of arbitrary power, the consequences do follow through judicial process. After all, the distribution of natural resources should contribute to the public good. As regards the two comparatively recent cases—the 2G spectrum case and the coal allocations case—which were decided by the Supreme Court, Harish Salve considers the judgements delivered therein to be legally flawed. He says with regard to the 2G spectrum judgement, 'This judgement, according to me, does not deal with the logic of the policy under which licences were granted at a preset price. It says you must auction spectrum—which is really a matter of policy. The trouble is that there is a trust deficit with the government, and I think this impacts upon and destroys policymaking in India. As a result, the court ends up micromanaging administration. No one defends corruption—if the court found corruption or arbitrariness in the process, it could have quashed the decisions tainted by their vice. To hold that a government must always maximize revenues has far-reaching implications in an emerging economy.'

About the judgement on coal allocations, Harish Salve's view is that it is wrong on many grounds. Criticism and healthy debates are the only viable way of refining and disseminating our thoughts on such matters, which helps in the development of law and creating new constitutional jurisprudence.

When one considers the professional chart of the seven lawyers about whom this wonderful book is written, there are different images that emerge, but if there is one thing which is common to them, it is that none of them has failed to live up to his promise. They have towered over the rest, deservedly, as they possess all the necessary elements for succeeding in the profession—skill in argument, perception of legal principles, close train of logic, command over language and eloquence. For me, personally, it was always a delight to hear them argue.

Leading lawyers, as they are, must now take the lead in court reforms, particularly with regard to the reduction of time in oral arguments—seeing that the Supreme Court has developed a crushing backlog of cases. The time has come for slashing the time taken for oral arguments and allowing the court to set new parameters.

Indu Bhan's work will fascinate all those who want to gain an intimate view of individuals who have contributed to the advancement of law in their own way in the last two decades or so. The author takes the reader along while drawing biographical sketches of the legal eagles and, in the process, she examines with an open, inquiring gaze the secret of their success in the profession. The work is splendid.

R.M. LODHA
Former Chief Justice of India

AUTHOR'S NOTE

If there was a toolkit to success . . . who wouldn't buy one or perhaps two?

Legal Eagles is about seven winners.

It gives me immense pride in presenting before you some of these 'big' legal luminaries who have helped shape the legal landscape of modern India. With its prime focus on legal aspects, this book touches upon and explores some of the most pressing issues of our times.

These legal celebrities are lively and vibrant in their own respective ways. They are real people like you and me. Like all of us, they too have their own flaws, foibles and insecurities. But then, like all of us, they are also prone to negative energy. Like all of us, they too have their own desires, dreams and aspirations. The only difference is that they are all involved, at all times, in high-profile matters.

But I have made an attempt to analyse some of their positive qualities. By this I mean the finer shades of their personalities, their nuances—not the darker side of their personalities—and what emerges, which can best be summed up as their perseverance, their dedication, the perfection in their preparation method and the finesse with which they carry out their tasks.

The significant six—except Justice Rohinton Nariman—are also amongst the most highly paid professionals in the country today. Apart from commanding a five-figure fee for a single court appearance, owning big luxury cars, business-class travel and five-star accommodations are all de rigueur. But all of this is fully justified! For every big company, these lawyers amount to must-have legal counsel.

But merely emulating, imbibing and practising the way these people conducted themselves will not take you to those higher levels. You need to go a step ahead . . . further and further . . . to recognize the calibre in you. And at no point should you forget Lady Luck.

Volumes can be written about them. But my intention is not to go through legal complexities with a fine-tooth comb, nor to embark on a mind-boggling academic analysis of the law. The intention is for this volume to be a pleasant reading experience and, ideally, to be a source of inspiration for aspiring lawyers.

Legal Eagles comprises crisp and engaging life-sketches of seven winners—how they started on their personal journeys, where they are now, what they were earlier and what they have now become.

The selected seven were not construed to be role models for the purposes of this book. The 'winners' explore and answer questions about certain basic tenets of the legal profession through their personal experiences. *Legal Eagles* embraces nearly five decades of their vast and rich experience. They have touched upon factors such as legal ethics, court craft and the craftiness required of an ideal lawyer. They talk about cases, their court preparation and their style and delivery of arguments.

'Winners' abound in the legal profession. Why these seven? The question is a valid one.

When the idea of *Legal Eagles* started taking shape, a wide list of lawyers came to my mind. All are equally eminent. I consulted a large number of lawyers, both juniors and seniors as well as retired judges, before arriving at these seven.

Their selection is neither random, nor the result of a careful exercise of separating the men from the boys. Surely, there are more celebrated lawyers. And their list is doubtless long. I do not have the wisdom to be a judge of their competence either.

There are a few common threads in these select few, however. One, it can be said that they have been *the* lawyers to watch out for in the post-liberalization era. But then this is not a list of successful lawyers. Look at any noteworthy corporate disputes or constitutional issues post 1991, and one will be able to see the indelible mark of one or more of these seven.

The second common thread is that they represent a new generation of greatness after the era of eminent lawyers like P. Parasaran, Ram Jethmalani, Fali Nariman, Soli Sorabjee, Shanti Bhushan, Ashok Desai, P.P. Rao, K.K. Venugopal, and so on. I haven't had the good fortune of seeing these masters at work in their golden period, I have just seen a glimpse. These magnificent seven have worthily replaced the fabled old guard.

I drew up my list based on what I saw as a journalist for years together, and after studying the feedback from my other counterparts, I left out certain names which were a part of the government. Much has transpired since I started writing this book. I had to leave out of this mix various lawyers-turned-politicians-turned-lawyers who are also doing extremely well at present. When I embarked on my endeavour, senior lawyers like Kapil Sibal and P. Chidambaram were still ministers in the United Progressive Alliance (UPA) government. They didn't practise then.

I have one regret though. Being a woman myself, I wasn't able to include a woman lawyer.

There may be omissions, but they are not intentional.

I present *Legal Eagles* with no prejudice.

I

HARISH SALVE: THE INVINCIBLE

Born on 22 June 1956 in Nagpur

Success is not final, failure is not fatal:
It is the courage to continue that counts
—Sir Winston Churchill

HARISH SALVE had just crossed his teens and, as a young film enthusiast, he was completely floored and absolutely bewitched by the charms of his Bollywood idol. He was enthralled by this towering personality that he would hear speak, enchanted by his personality, his charm, his aura. There was something unusual and magnetic about him that attracted people.

That actor was Dilip Kumar.

Spellbound by his charisma, young Harish, who had already developed a passion for taxation and the law, would sit all day and hear the discussions carefully, with the occasional— incisive—interjection.

'My father led the team, and we had meetings all day, well into the evening, when the sun disappeared into the Arabian Sea. It was absolutely mesmerizing,' says Harish, now one of India's top lawyers and a mature, successful and equally charismatic man, describing his initial tryst with law, and his first opinion of the towering personality that thespian actor Dilip Kumar was.

Dilip Kumar, also known as the Hindi film industry's tragedy king, would sit all day to witness the discussion for his case—*Income Tax Officer v. Dilip Kumar alias Yousuf Khan*—that was being heard by the income tax tribunal on a day-to-day basis in June 1975.

Harish reminisces, 'I would sit quietly, listening to the discussion headed by my father, N.K.P. Salve [later a Union minister and president of the Board of Control for Cricket in India (BCCI)], advising his client to fight and contest the appeal in the income-tax tribunal.' The other members in the team included Ajay Thakore, advocate and tax consultant par excellence, and G.N. Joshi, the client's trusted chartered accountant.

The team would sit in a suite at the Oberoi Hotel at Nariman Point in Mumbai. They met for almost two continuous weeks in June 1975. Harish had just graduated in May 1975, and his father had allowed him to 'carry his files' to the tribunal. This was to be one of India's most famous lawyer's first involvement with the law, his first case and, as he himself admits, probably one of his most memorable ones.

The story does not end there. 'I appeared for the matinee idol—Dilip Kumar—at the Supreme Court. It was the day I got my *sanad* [the enrolment licence that enables one to practise in court]. From the tax tribunal, the case wound its way up to the Supreme Court, where I appeared for the legendary actor in an appeal filed by the tax department,' says Harish.

The Background

As a young boy, Harish wanted to be an engineer. By the time he was ready for college, he was deeply interested in chartered accountancy, wanting to follow in his father's footsteps. 'My father, however, had given up accountancy and did only income tax matters. This brought him in close proximity to the one and only Nani Palkhivala—perhaps the greatest advocate the country has ever known,' says Harish.

From the late 1950s, Palkhivala used to appear frequently in tax cases and was often briefed by Harish's father. 'I remember that I was busy preparing for the chartered accountancy final exam, when my father requested me to prepare a note on some complicated point in relation to the new provisions establishing the Settlement Commission.' His father was deeply impressed by the note and decided to show it to Palkhivala, whose opinion was being sought by the client. 'When this note was shown to him, he asked, "So when are you joining the profession?"' Harish remembers fondly. The penny had dropped!

It was Palkhivala who inspired Harish to take up the study of the law. He soon lost interest in accountancy and became interested in tax matters. His interest grew deeper, and he decided that if he wanted to practise taxation, then he should opt to become a lawyer.

Born in Nagpur, he went to SFS School, which was established by the Missionaries of St Francis de Sales in 1870. After graduating in commerce from Nagpur University, he studied law and chartered accountancy simultaneously. 'My grandfather was a successful criminal lawyer. My father, N.K.P. Salve, was an eminent chartered accountant practising in Nagpur. My mother, Ambriti Salve, was a doctor. So at a very early age, I imbibed professional qualities and values from the two professionals at home,' Harish says, talking about the importance of being professional.

Harish grew up in a tier-two town, where life was uncomplicated. Fun was defined as visits to the neighbouring forests, or discussing anything and everything with friends over endless cups of tea. Alcohol was an occasional luxury. It was a matter of privilege if one got to drink a bottle or two of beer. Dinners with friends were enjoyed the most, especially at dhabas, eating alongside truck drivers. 'Although we have stopped visiting roadside dhabas, we still find the time to socialize. I also have a group of a few close friends whom I have known for the last three decades since I moved to Delhi. But no one from the legal profession,' Harish says, fondly remembering his time with his friends.

Nagpur in those days used to be a quiet city, and so was life—quiet and serene. All Harish remembers of his college days in the small city was going to college to break the spell of monotony and serenity. College was a happening place, and Harish would always return recharged. 'Fortunately, I did well in college and was rewarded by being allowed to use the family car to drive out to the Melghat Tiger Reserve in Maharashtra,' Harish reminisces.

Those car journeys made all the difference. 'I enjoyed every bit of that drive; every passing moment would nurture something in me. Whether it was a long drive or a short one, it was always a significant one,' Harish says.

Melghat, located in the Amaravati district of Maharashtra, means 'a meeting of the ghats'. For Harish, confronting these large tracts of unending hills, ravines and steep climbs was like confronting the challenges posed by nature.

'It has been an unforgettable journey for me, a journey that brought to the forefront the mysteries and unforgiving laws of nature and the jungle. Melghat, the land of Project Tiger, where the king of the jungle lived alongside his prey, was testimony to the law of the survival of the fittest and the laws of nature which have no mercy,' says Harish.

What Harish thought would be the end of the journey, in fact, proved to be the beginning. That there are many facets of the law is something that he imbibed in this significant journey. 'Youngsters of my generation were no strangers to forests and nature, but this was at a different level,' says Harish.

This passion has driven him to tirelessly battle in the *Environment and Forest Conservation* cases as amicus curiae for almost the last two decades.

His Tryst with the Law

Harish had failed his chartered accountancy exams twice. 'Failure teaches you more in life than success does. Dealing with success is easy; accepting disappointments with equanimity and harnessing the energy of failure to achieve greater heights are the greatest lessons in life,' he says.

Harish felt that he must explore and take some risks doing other things. 'I wanted to start my independent practice. In 1980, I got myself enrolled with the Bar Council of Delhi and decided to move away from accountancy, because though I felt doing chartered accountancy was good education, it was not a profession I saw myself pursuing,' Harish says.

However, opposition came from extremely unusual quarters. Harish's father was not happy with his son's decision to join the Bar. He wanted Harish to look after Salve & Co., the reputed chartered accountancy firm set up by him in Nagpur. 'I had worked for Salve & Co. I did my articles with them, and even passed my chartered accountancy exam while working at the firm. My father wanted me to do taxation laws as he felt that it would be within my comfort zone in the family-run firm,' he said.

Harish's first day in office was as an article clerk in a chartered accountant firm in Nagpur. It was quite an experience sitting all day at work, with the background music of clattering typewriters, checking the totalling of ledgers written in Hindi. 'For me, it was more of a culture shock after coming from a missionary school. I had just passed school and joined college. I was quite reluctant to do the work assigned to me, but the idea that at the end of the month I would earn a stipend of Rs 50 made it all worthwhile,' Harish says, reminiscing about the days when even Rs 50 was a handsome amount in a city like Nagpur—it paid the tea and cigarette bills!

In 1978, Harish decided to relocate to Delhi to try his luck by setting up his practice at the Supreme Court, and joined J.B. Dadachandji & Co. as an intern. It was at this time that he got an opportunity to assist Palkhivala in the *Minerva Mills* case (*Minerva Mills Ltd v. Union of India*, AIR 1980 SC 1789). Later, in 1980, it was Palkhivala who suggested that Harish join the chambers of senior counsel Soli Sorabjee, who later became the Attorney General of India in April 1991. After that, there was no looking back. 'Being a chartered accountant and being exposed to commercial matters, I had a natural advantage in picking up the nuances of a tax or commercial-law brief. My senior, Soli Sorabjee, was an eminent jurist with an encyclopaedic knowledge of the law—but he hated figures. I got an opportunity to assist him in important cases and, later on, to argue a number of important matters under his guidance,' he said.

His First Case

Harish believes his legal career began when he assisted his father in 1975 in Dilip Kumar's case. The department had assessed Kumar on allegations of having earned black money, something for which Bollywood was notorious. The revenue authorities demanded not only tax but also penalties equal to the escaped income. Dilip Kumar potentially faced prosecution for tax evasion. Kumar won at the tribunal, but the reference was rejected. The Bombay High Court refused to call for a reference, and the department filed an appeal in the Supreme Court.

'I followed and represented Dilip Kumar in the Supreme Court. It took the judges barely forty-five seconds to throw out the appeal. Dilip Kumar was a very dear family friend. He was very happy. If I had to argue, I don't think I would have found my voice. Fortunately, I was not called upon to do so by the apex court,' says Harish, remembering his shy first days.

Bearer Bonds: The Real Challenge

It was a moment of pride, a challenge that Harish confronted with trepidation. It was one of the most 'telling events' of his life when he was made to argue before a five-judge Constitution Bench at the Supreme Court in the important Bearer Bonds case (*R.K. Garg v. Union of India* (1981) 4 SCC 675). 'I feel proud that I was associated with the landmark judgement. I think this matter established me as a lawyer. I was noticed and appreciated for my work by several senior lawyers,' Harish says with pride.

Bearer bonds were introduced and issued by the government. The issue involved converting cash into bearer bonds, like black money into white. 'I strongly felt that it was the wrong move. It was my gut feeling that made me approach Sorabjee to file a PIL [public interest litigation] to counter the government's move. I was working in Sorabjee's chamber when the issue of bearer bonds came to the forefront. Soli supported the issue and asked me to draft a PIL,' Harish says.

Eminent lawyer R.K. Garg too filed a PIL to this effect. The matter was heard by a Constitution Bench presided over by the then Chief Justice of India Y.V. Chandrachud as well as other judges including Justices P.N. Bhagwati, S. Murtaza Fazal Ali and A.C. Gupta. Sorabjee was to argue the case. Garg took the lead and argued the case first as Sorabjee was away at Srinagar to defend a challenge to the anti-defection law of Jammu and Kashmir. Garg argued for three hours. Being a great constitutional lawyer, he focused mostly on constitutional philosophy, but did not dwell on the legislative act—the Special Bearer Bonds (Immunities and Exemptions) Act, 1981—that was under challenge.

It appeared to Harish that the judges were not accepting Garg's arguments. 'Then my turn came around noon, and the judges wanted me to finish within an hour. As I was a raw junior, arguing before the Constitution Bench was a big thing for me. For the first few minutes, I lost my voice. Justice Chandrachud, though usually very encouraging to juniors, seemed to be hardly interested in listening to my arguments,' says Harish, relating the happenings of what was one of the most memorable days of his legal career.

Despite his nervousness, Harish began his arguments and, sharp at 1 p.m., Justice Chandrachud asked if he was done. To Harish's surprise and relief, Justice Bhagwati interjected, 'You heard Garg for three days. This young man is making fine points. He should be allowed to argue till he wants,' and he was warmly supported by Justice A.C. Gupta. Chief Justice Chandrachud yielded immediately to his brother judges, and Harish continued arguing till 4 p.m.

'When I had finished, I think I got the greatest tribute from the then Attorney General Mr L.N. Sinha, a giant whom I hero-worshipped. He got up and said, "I can counter Garg's points in fifteen minutes, but I have heard the young man with fascination. I will ask my friend Mr Parasaran [the then Solicitor General] to first try and answer this young man's submissions." I was overwhelmed at the warmth and affection I received from a revered senior like Mr Sinha,' says Harish, remembering the day fondly.

By the time they had to rejoin, Sorabjee was back in Delhi, but wanted Harish to address the court. He deliberately came late, sat next to Harish and guided him through the proceedings. 'I was so tense for my rejoinder that I got fever the night before. We lost by 4:1. But Justice Gupta dissented in my favour. He analysed and accepted my arguments and criticized the majority judgement!' Harish says.

The majority judgement stated: 'Laws relating to economic activities should be viewed with greater latitude than laws touching civil rights such as freedom of speech, religion, etc. The court—after reviewing past decisions—said that on the issue of economic regulation, courts must give considerable leeway to the legislature. It is a fundamental rule that the duty of judges is to expound and not legislate.'

Becoming a Senior Advocate

Harish was designated as a senior advocate by the Delhi High Court in 1992. 'I am fortunate to have the opportunity to appear in important cases involving corporate bigwigs like the Ambanis, the Mahindras, several Tata companies as well as representing Ratan Tata in his right to privacy matter,' says Harish.

He has been frequently representing large companies like Mukesh Ambani's Reliance Industries Limited (RIL) in big-ticket cases like the *Krishna–Godavari Basin Gas Dispute* case against his younger brother Anil Ambani's Reliance Natural Resources Limited (RNRL). The Reliance empire was split vertically between the two brothers, who then fought over the gas project. Anil Ambani–owned RNRL had cited a 2005 family pact claiming it had rights to obtain gas from the Mukesh Ambani–led RIL for seventeen years at the rate of $2.34 per MMBtu (million British thermal unit). While the Bombay High Court had decided in favour of the younger brother, Anil, the Supreme Court finally settled the matter by saying that the government owns the natural resource (gas) till 'it reaches its ultimate consumer, and parties must restrict their negotiation within the conditions of the government policy'.

'I thought it was a relatively simple matter. But the media hype and other factors led to problems. I also realized that unlike the matured economies, where the written word of the contract has the highest sanctity, in India, each judge will superimpose his sense of justice—even if it means reworking the written contract,' says Harish.

Harish also defended Keshub Mahindra in the *Union Carbide* case when the government filed a curative petition seeking a review of the apex court's verdict dated 13 September 1996 in the *Bhopal Gas Tragedy* case. By that verdict, the apex court had quashed the framing of charges against Mahindra and six other senior officials of Union Carbide India for committing culpable homicide not amounting to murder, which attracted a maximum imprisonment of ten years. The government argued that the *Bhopal Gas Tragedy* case fell in the category of the rarest of rare cases, and that the court must remove all obstacles so that the perpetrators of the disaster get punishment in tune with their crime.

'I took the stand that the curative petition was not maintainable, as the Supreme Court had, in 1996, decided the issue on merits, and it could not be revisited now so as to revive culpable homicide charges,' reminisces Harish.

His other noteworthy clients include former Tata group chairman Ratan Tata, who had approached the Supreme Court against the alleged violation of his right to privacy brought about by the publication of the Niira Radia tapes by two magazines. It was a privacy petition concerning the leakage and publication of the conversations of corporate lobbyist Niira Radia, recorded by the income tax department, which exposed an alleged politico-corporate crony capitalistic nexus, causing a huge scandal in late 2010.

Then there was the case that shook up the political and corporate classes alike. It was the mammoth $2.5 billion *Vodafone* case. Winning it turned Harish into an almost-invincible lawyer. People started viewing him as one who could win the impossible for any client he took on. In a landmark decision, the Supreme Court reversed the decision of the Bombay High Court and held that the Indian tax authorities did not have territorial jurisdiction to tax the offshore transaction and, therefore, Vodafone was not liable to withhold Indian taxes. 'I kept a picture of Palkhivala in front of me throughout the time I prepared for the case, because he is such a great inspirational figure to me,' Harish says.

The other important cases that Harish handled include representing the Delhi Police in the matter concerning yoga guru

Baba Ramdev, who was protesting against corruption; Harish's defence led to Ramdev's indictment as well.

Harish also represented the Italian Embassy and defended its two marines, who were charged with killing two fishermen off the Kerala coast. Later, he withdrew from the case when the Italian government threatened not to return the marines.

It is Harish's success stories that have made him the first choice for litigants. Of all his successful ventures, Harish considers the *Bilkis Bano* case as a major triumph, as this resulted in the apex court ordering a Central Bureau of Investigation (CBI) inquiry into the killing of a family of a poor lady—at a time when Gujarat was plagued by communal violence.

Amicus Curiae

Harish was appointed as amicus curiae by the Supreme Court in several notable cases including the *Environmental and Forest Conservation* cases and the *Delhi Vehicular Pollution* case.

'Amicus curiae', in literal terms, means 'a friend of the court'. In India, while handling cases of high public interest, the courts have often appointed senior advocates with impeccable integrity as amicus curiae. The job of an amicus is to assist the court with an objective and impartial analysis of the matter, so that justice is served and public interest prevails. 'In my capacity as an amicus, I have assisted the court in setting up a system that would try to ensure justice to the victims,' he says.

Harish was also appointed the amicus by the Supreme Court in another case related to the Gujarat riots. But the case generated lot of heat, with riot victims accusing him of professional misconduct and working against public interest. The lawyers—Kamini Jaiswal and Prashant Bhushan—alleged that Harish, besides being an amicus in the riot cases, where

the Gujarat government is a suspect, has been defending some
tainted policemen in another case. Despite this accusation,
the three-judge bench of Justices D.K. Jain, P. Sathasivam
(currently the governor of Kerala) and Aftab Alam overruled
them, saying, 'It's not your faith which matters. We have full
faith in Salve's impartiality.' And so Harish continued to be the
amicus.

A Memorable Moment

It was in 2001 that there was a widespread stir in the NCR
region of Delhi. People were not happy with the government
introducing compressed natural gas (CNG) for automobiles.
Public inconvenience and a lack of infrastructure were perhaps
the main reasons for this unrest. However, the larger problem of
health issues was missed out on.

While sitting in Chief Justice J.S. Verma's courtroom,
Harish was asked by him to assist the court in M.C. Mehta's
petition relating to automobile pollution. The court directed
the Government of India to appoint a statutory authority.
This authority recommended shifting all the buses in Delhi to
the CNG model. While the Centre and Delhi government
agreed to do this, when the time came, they reneged on their
stand.

These events constitute one of Harish's most memorable
experiences, which involved getting the Supreme Court to force
the Delhi government to switch to CNG amidst widespread
protests from all kinds of people. Not only did the Supreme Court
come under criticism, even Harish was personally attacked for the
unyielding stand taken by him as amicus curiae. However, history
has vindicated the Supreme Court. 'My concern was only to take
effective measures to introduce clean fuels,' he says.

As a Lawyer

As a young lawyer, Harish learnt a great amount from working with Palkhivala. 'I owe a lot to the genius. He has been my idol,' says Harish. Fondly remembering the days spent as a junior working for the legendary lawyer, Harish relates this incident that forms one of the most pleasant memories of those days. 'It so happened that a client once took my opinion in a very complex tax-related matter and then went on to test it by asking Palkhivala to examine it. After scrutinizing the complexity therein, my guru, Palkhivala, said, "I have nothing more to add to Harish's opinion." Sometimes, happiness can be found in such small things.'

Palkhivala taught Harish to make excellence an end unto itself. He would often tell Harish, then a budding lawyer, that the measure of how well you've argued in court comes not from the decision of the court, but from how you personally feel you've performed. 'From him, I learnt that genius is a lot of hard work. It entails having the capacity to do what people find boring—that is where you hone your attention to detail. He opened up a whole new dimension of the world to me,' says Harish.

Like other successful lawyers, Harish also values rigorous preparation and firmly believes that spontaneity is what distinguishes a good counsel from a not-so-good one. How one counsels the client and what advice one gives makes a lot of difference. Harish, through the vast experience he has now accumulated, seems to have mastered this art of counselling, which in a way distinguishes him from several other leading lawyers.

'Harish has been successful because he is very convincing and never seems to be forcing his view on the judge,' says one of his colleagues who has seen him grow since 1980. Senior Supreme Court lawyer K.K. Venugopal says, 'He is the foremost counsel of his generation. Law is a great passion for him. No one works at his craft like he does.' Shanti Bhushan, another octogenarian top constitutional lawyer, also has words of praise: 'Harish is competent and possesses excellent court-craft, but lacks comprehensive constitutional knowledge.'

Raian Karanjawala, managing partner of Karanjawala & Co., the law firm that engaged Harish on Ratan Tata's behalf, says, 'Harish can talk to any client, no matter how big, as an equal. He commands respect and confidence in courts, and his court craft is superb.'

Harish is greatly appreciated and respected in corporate circles as well. 'Harish is very committed and client-friendly. He is passionate about protecting his client's interests,' said another lawyer who often engages Harish for a top telecom company.

Many corporate lawyers speak of Harish's work ethic and his insistence on understanding a complex issue. Harish once took half a day to simply understand the functioning of a refinery, and even sat through an eight-hour conference, taking only one break. 'Harish's razor-sharp mind and court presence is well known. But what I find amazing about him is his breadth of knowledge. He is as comfortable with accounting issues as he is with engineering issues as well as constitutional issues. His commercial understanding of legal issues is outstanding. He is technologically way ahead of his peers. But most importantly, he is a good human being who loves his profession and gives it everything. He is an inspiration to us all,' says Sameer Parekh, the managing partner at Parekh & Co., who often briefs Harish in high-stake matters including those concerning RIL.

Harish's great advantage is that he makes his high-profile clients feel comfortable. 'Harish has an encyclopaedic knowledge of the diverse avenues of law, be it arbitration, banking, constitutional, taxation matters, etc. This gives him an unparalleled edge in advising and dealing with complex matters with the utmost ease,' says Mahesh Agarwal of Agarwal Associates, which represents Anil Ambani's group companies at the Supreme Court.

Corporate lawyers talk of Harish's ability to be impressive without being intimidating in any courtroom. 'He's very persuasive. He skilfully judges what a judge will listen to. What persuades big clients to go for him is that he is always forthright when it comes to speaking on policy and politics,' says Karanjawala.

Harish is a firm believer that the Indian state often victimizes entrepreneurship. He is clear and frank in his assessment that many telecom cases make little sense. 'Sunil Mittal, founder and chairman, Bharti Enterprises, put Indian telecom on the world map, and now you treat him like a criminal,' argues Harish. 'I feel there's a self-defeating war against business and businessmen. If every businessman is supposed to be dishonest . . . a crook . . . well, then jail everybody,' he says, exasperated with the current attitude towards conducting business in India.

Harish makes it a point to apprise his clients and advise the best for them in a particular case. 'I never advise my corporate clients to litigate at every possible chance. I tell them to settle whenever they can . . . Also, I never take a case unless I am in possession of all the facts . . . I mean all the facts,' he says. There are many foreign investors who consult him in their fact-finding missions in India.

While generally praising the Supreme Court for its judgements, Harish faults the court for the treatment meted out to commercial law and arbitration law in particular. Harish says, 'There are judgements which should have been subjected to more research and analysis. I think we do not have an arbitration mindset. Some of the judgements on arbitration law virtually make arbitrations meaningless. The Supreme Court has, in my opinion, mishandled arbitration law at times.'

He is also critical of the 2G spectrum judgement delivered by a bench headed by Justice G.S. Singhvi in February 2012. He says the judgement is 'flawed'. The Supreme Court cancelled 122 licences allotted on or after 10 January 2008 to eleven companies during the tenure of the former telecom minister, A. Raja. It further held that spectrum, being a scarce natural resource, 'is vested with the government as a matter of trust in the name of the people of India, and it is the solemn duty of the state to protect the national interest, and natural resources must always be used in the interests of the country and not private interests'. He goes on, 'This judgement, according to me, does not deal with the logic of the policy under which licences were granted at a preset price. It says you must auction spectrum—which is really a matter of policy. The trouble is that there is a trust deficit with the government, and I think this impacts upon and destroys policymaking in India. As a result, the court ends up micromanaging administration. No one defends corruption—if the court found corruption or arbitrariness in the process, it could have quashed the decisions tainted by their vice. To hold that a government must always maximize revenues has far-reaching implications in an emerging economy.'

He disagrees with the judgement on the coal scam as well. 'I strongly feel that the coal order is wrong on many grounds. In my view, the judgement misreads the definition of a government company by confining it only to a central government undertaking. The judgement also has an inconsistency . . . On the one hand, it says the state government continues to play a role under the Mines and Minerals (Regulation and Development) Amendment Act, and yet it accepted that the letters of allocation given by the Union government were valuable. Thirdly, the judgement does not address the point which I raised . . . There were companies who applied for a coal mine, gave all the material and documents to justify their demand. The screening committee allotted the mine, but did not record their reasons properly. If the court found fault with the committee, it could have allowed the allottee to place before it the same material it had placed before the Government of India. Not hearing the allottees caused a miscarriage of justice in some cases.' In Harish's view, the courts sometimes act as they do on account of the huge trust deficit in the governments of the day.

As the Solicitor General

Harish took over as the Solicitor General of India (SG) in 1999 during the National Democratic Alliance (NDA) regime. He was only forty-three at the time, and held office till 2002. 'My stint as the SG was special and quite educational. It made me understand the problems of the government. I think understanding government machinery is a sensitive issue, and one can grasp it better if one works in a government set-up. It makes you a more rounded lawyer,' he says.

As the SG, Harish handled several important cases on behalf of the government. The *Tamil Nadu Water Dispute* case was an important matter where Karnataka refused to open water channels of the Cauvery river for Tamil Nadu's use. An order of contempt was issued by the Supreme Court against the then Karnataka chief minister S.M. Krishna's defiance of its earlier orders in the Cauvery issue in not releasing a certain amount of water to Tamil Nadu. The Supreme Court had taken a very serious view of this and had issued a notice of contempt to the state of Karnataka. Tamil Nadu wanted Karnataka to pay damages to it for the loss of crops estimated at Rs 2930 crore.

'As Solicitor General, I was asked to inform the court as to what should be done when a state government wilfully disobeyed the orders of the apex court,' relates Harish. 'I remember it was a Friday, and I wanted time till Monday. I sent a request to the chief minister [S.M. Krishna] to meet me. He came in the evening. I said, "Mr Krishna, you can rescue Indian federalism." "There is something wrong with the interim order," he said. I said, "I will help you get the interim order corrected, but first your government should respect the order of the court."'

Harish continues, 'I said, "All of the water is not going to flow out over the weekend. Once you get the interim order corrected, you can always close the gates." He agreed and said, "I will open the gates tomorrow." On Saturday morning, he had all the gates opened. On Sunday, the heavens opened up and it rained and rained! By Monday, Tamil Nadu was asking Karnataka to close the gates because too much water was coming down. And Monday, at 2 p.m., when the Supreme Court took up the case, I told the judges I must salute the CM. He rose above politics and put nationalism on the forefront. In the evening, the CM sent me a bouquet of flowers.'

As the second-topmost law officer for the Union of India, Harish conducted a large number of important matters like the first anti-dumping case which was argued in the Supreme Court, and the first case of privatization of public sector undertakings (PSUs), the Balco case. He was also involved in important non-litigation work such as helping in the World Trade Organization (WTO) negotiations, helping in the drafting the electricity reforms, etc.

Harish had a wonderful tenure as the SG of India. 'I will always remember the affection and support I got from former prime minister Atal Behari Vajpayee, BJP [Bharatiya Janata Party] leaders L.K. Advani, Union minister Sushma Swaraj, my dear friend Arun Jaitley, now the Minister of Finance of the country, Dr Murli Manohar Joshi, Mr Anant Kumar, Mr Suresh Prabhu, and so many others,' he reminisces fondly.

Blackstone Chambers

Harish decided to join London's Blackstone Chambers to become an English barrister. He was called to join Gray's Inn—one of four London Inns of Courts that barristers are required to join before they can practise before courts in England and Wales.

They have a very flexible system for the admissions process for foreign lawyers. While qualifications are 'undoubtedly important' in the process, the English Bar also takes into account one's 'overall credentials'. The general rule to become a barrister in England and Wales requires that budding practitioners undertake a 'pupilage' under a senior lawyer, but in 'exceptional cases' this could be waived by the regulators.

'I had to fulfil some of the ceremonial requirements, which includes literally dining with the other members of the Inns. I feel very happy about joining Blackstone. It is a different world! Blackstone Chambers has some of the finest legal talent. On a personal level, all the members are extremely affable—there is a great informality in the interpersonal interactions. There are professionals who are always ready to help each other, and I feel privileged that I got an opportunity to sit in a room that was for decades occupied by the famous Michael Beloff, QC.'

In contrast, there is a lot of domestic opposition to the entry of foreign lawyers into India. Harish feels there is a lobby holding things up and it is not interested in getting the domestic market liberalized. Ironically, there are professionals from this lobby who have signed best-friend agreements with some of these foreign firms. In an increasingly shrinking world, where India is going to be a significant economic player, Harish is of the opinion that it's important that we come together and work together. He has kept his base as Delhi despite taking up tenancy at the London chambers. He is now engaged with a lot of international work by way of international arbitrations including bilateral treaty obligations. He is at present working on building a practice in the commercial courts.

A Typical Day

A typical working day for one of India's most successful lawyers could begin any time from 7.45 a.m. to 10 a.m. and go on until 7 p.m. On days when court hearings are scheduled, it starts really early. On other days when only reading and meetings are scheduled, it's more relaxed. 'After a long time, I am thoroughly enjoying working in the area of commercial law. I now realize how much India has to catch up in the culture of commercial law—and I am afraid that unless we do that, it will always be a negative against India as a destination for FDI [foreign direct investment],' Harish says.

He firmly believes that a modern lawyer has to be a lean, mean fighting machine—a service provider par excellence, well trained in his area of speciality. Service to the client has to be measured in clear terms—one no longer has the luxury of bullying clients or pulling off second-class service at top-dollar prices. One's skills, qualities and strategies are integral to success. One such important quality is that of court craft.

Also, when a case comes up in court, Harish lives and breathes that matter. He gives up all other petitions. 'I attend court daily to hear the other side's arguments. I don't like to distract myself and prefer to concentrate on the case at hand. You never know when a new idea pops up,' he says.

When he isn't knee-deep in a case, Harish loves reading on a wide variety of topics apart from the law. 'I am most inspired by Churchill's' narrative of the Second World War,' he says. He also likes spending time with his wife, Meenakshi, a stained-glass designer, and with his daughters, his best buddies—Sakshi and Saaniya. To unwind, Harish often spends time in the family parlour at his residence in Delhi's Vasant Vihar, playing the piano. He has a passion for music, and is fond of listening to Cuban jazz pianist Gonzalo Rubalcaba. Harish is a connoisseur of art, and every little artefact in his house has sentimental value.

In his quieter moments he often remembers his mother. In her memory, Harish has set up a scholarship at Exeter College, Oxford.

Hall of Legal Fame

Harish Salve is simple and modest at heart, but a thorough professional as well—the perfect role model for budding young lawyers. For him, professionals are all 'students of law', and can and are entitled to make mistakes. Mistakes are not bad; dedication and sincerity are the most important attributes that a professional can have, according to him.

Harish's views on his personal wealth are also refreshing. 'One thing I've learnt is to never be apologetic about success. I have earned it through my hard work. I haven't stood on anybody's grave to get to where I've got,' he says, and adds that one must enjoy the results of the hard work too.

'For something to be convincing, it must in the first place be simple,' is what Palkhivala termed Churchill's art of persuasion. Harish is a firm believer in this, and would like to extend this advice to all fellow professionals.

Harish may have climbed heights and received accolades, but there are certain simple things that have made him a prominent figure in the Hall of Legal Fame.

Unforgettable is his rational approach that professionals must focus on how they can present complex legal propositions with clarity and simplicity to help the judges comprehend and assimilate the arguments that are being made. He has a positive outlook on life, and is very particular about his personal fitness. He is very regular and extremely particular with his cardio and workout regime. He feels that there has to be a change in the mindset and one must tell one's body that you love it the most and give it at least one hour of your time every day. He looks slim and trim and feels 'fitter today than he was at thirty-five'.

If the body is healthy, the mind will be sharp, and you will be able to accomplish much more in your professional life. This is something Harish believes in. He further emphasizes on this point, saying, 'You must cut down on work if you can't find the time to give to your body. Professionals must live a disciplined life in which they sleep early and get up early and do a rigorous workout.'

Harish is a lawyer par excellence, and has been ranked amongst the most powerful persons in the country today. Harish was conferred the Padma Bhushan, the country's third-highest civilian honour on Republic Day in 2015.

An 'activist' court is no substitute for good government, but at the same time, the judicial arm of social reform (as Justice P.N. Bhagwati referred to the Supreme Court) cannot be a mute spectator to rampant executive apathy and violation of constitutional norms.

THE CASE

Vodafone International Holdings B.V. v. Union of India, Civil Appeal No. 733 of 2012.

Judgement delivered on 20 January 2012 by bench comprising Chief Justice of India S.H. Kapadia, and Justices K.S. Radhakrishnan and Swatanter Kumar.

Case Details

British telecom operator Vodafone's tax dispute with the Government of India has gone down the annals of Indian legal history for all its intricacies and the strong bearing it had on Indian business, economy and politics. After the reign of the East India Company, it is only a few overseas firms that have influenced the collective Indian intellectual psyche as much as Vodafone.

For the very complex nature of the tax row, the *Vodafone* case at the very beginning itself had shown the signs that it would assume hitherto unforeseen significance. And it did. During the course of the case, the controversy took many twists and turns and, it can arguably claim, in the process it changed the perceptions of business and politics in India.

Eyeing a large slice of the then fast-growing telecom market in India, British telecom giant Vodafone bought a 67 per cent stake in Hutchison Telecommunications International Ltd's (HTIL) Indian operations, Hutchison Essar (HEL), for over $11.2 billion. The deal was the biggest-ever acquisition in India in 2007, and was structured through complex layers of overseas subsidiaries of both the companies, but routed through the Cayman Islands, a tax haven.

In February 2007, Vodafone International Holdings B.V, a Dutch entity, acquired 100 per cent stake in CGP (Holdings) Ltd, a Cayman Islands company for $11.1 billion from HTIL. CGP held a 67 per cent in HEL, a joint venture between the Hutchison group and the Ruias–led Essar group. The acquisition resulted in Vodafone acquiring control over CGP and its downstream subsidiaries, including HEL.

The deal in the due course of time obtained necessary regulatory clearances. But the Indian income tax department had other ideas. Latching on to what some may in hindsight call a loophole in the laws, the tax department issued a show-cause notice to Vodafone under Section 201 of the Income Tax Act, 1961 (the IT Act), stating that the company did not deduct capital gains tax from the payment made to HTIL. The revenue authorities pegged the tax at $2 billion. This was only the beginning of a long and highly intensely fought court battle that reverberated in the Indian Parliament later.

Strengthening its grounds, the IT department also decided to treat Vodafone as an agent of Hutch, a non-resident, under Section 163 of the IT Act. It was a foregone conclusion that Vodafone would go to court. It filed a writ petition at the Bombay High Court, which dismissed Vodafone's plea in September 2010 and ruled that the assets located in India were transferred and that Vodafone is liable for the payment of taxes.

After the government emerged victorious, as its contentions prevailed, Vodafone moved the Supreme Court. Solicitor General Mohan Parasaran represented the government. Senior counsel Harish Salve was Vodafone's lawyer.

After hearing the arguments for a month or so, the Supreme Court in January 2012 reversed the decision of the Bombay High Court and held that the Indian tax authorities did not have territorial jurisdiction to tax the offshore transaction and, therefore, Vodafone was not liable to withhold Indian taxes. Vodafone won the case. The apex court in a majority judgement by Justices Kapadia and Swatanter Kumar held that the transaction took place between two overseas firms and there was no provision under Indian law to tax such deals. Even Justice Radhakrishnan gave a separate judgement, but concurred with the views of the Chief Justice of India on all major issues. The top court also directed the tax authorities to return Rs 2500 crore, which had been earlier deposited by Vodafone, along with 4 per cent interest, and to also return the bank guarantee of Rs 8500 crore.

It held that both Vodafone and Hutch were not 'fly by night' operators or short-term investors, and had contributed substantially—Rs 20,242 crore—to the exchequer between 2002–03 and 2010–11, by way of both direct and indirect taxes. Even the apex court asked the government to have clear tax laws to avoid conflicting views.

The Vodafone victory was hailed by one and all. It was a big boost to foreign investor sentiment. Companies that had entered into such similar deals breathed easy. Many thought the apex court order would act as a catalyst for foreign investments in India. Alas, the feel-good sentiment was short-lived.

The Supreme Court ruling also said that the government can amend the law to enable itself to rightfully tax such deals. The then government did exactly that by amending the law retrospectively in May 2012 to bring the indirect transfer of Indian assets by overseas companies under the tax department's purview, giving the department powers to revive its $11.08 billion tax demand on Vodafone.

Impact
The decision came as a big relief to international investors. The Supreme Court judgement had not only marked a closure to the tax demand on Vodafone, it also

had far-reaching ramifications on diverse cross-border transactions sought to be brought within the tax net by the Indian tax authorities.

At least eight other companies are facing similar litigation. Sanofi Aventis–Shantha Biotechnics, SABMiller–Foster's, Idea Cellular–AT&T, GE, Cadbury and Vedanta are among the companies fighting tax cases before different courts in India.

While the Supreme Court had acknowledged that certainty and stability were the basis of any fiscal system, the retrospective amendment, however, has not gone down well with everyone. Tax experts feel that any legislation has to be fair, commercial and realistic if one wants the financial environment to prosper, especially when India continues to remain an important destination for investors. Analysts feel that investors would think twice before investing billions in a country when the rules get revised later.

However, one thing is clear. While tax planning through offshore structures is permitted, foreign companies need to be vigilant when structuring investments into India through offshore intermediary companies located in tax havens like Mauritius, Singapore and Cyprus. They should identify potential risks and safeguarding measures before signing any offshore deals.

The government has also introduced general anti-avoidance rules (GAAR) to check tax evasion.

Winning Arguments

For all those who keenly followed the proceedings at the Bombay High Court and then in the Supreme Court, Harish was the real face of Vodafone.

The British firm took no chances and engaged Harish for the entire duration of the final twenty-six days before the Supreme Court. Harish argued for seventeen consecutive days on how Hutchison's structure was a genuine foreign investment and why the deal was not subject to capital gains tax.

As much as the *Vodafone* case will be remembered for its high stakes, for Harish too this is one case documenting his expertise as a tax lawyer, chartered accountant, constitutional lawyer and, above all, his advocacy skills.

'He was the team leader and, ultimately, he guided us in the case. To my mind, he is the best lawyer today, not only in India but amongst the top legal minds in the world,' says Anuradha Dutt, partner at Dutt Menon and Dunmorrsett, which handled the *Vodafone* case.

During the arguments before the Supreme Court, Harish meticulously took the judges through the deal and submitted that complex structures were designed not for avoiding tax but for good commercial reasons, and that the Indian legal structure and foreign exchange laws recognize Overseas Corporate Bodies (OCBs). Such transnational structures also contain exit options for the investors.

Harish pointed out that the tax residency certificate issued by the Mauritian authorities had to be respected, and in the absence of any limitation-on-benefit (LOB) clause, the benefit of the Indo-Mauritian treaty would be available to third parties who invested in India through the Mauritius route.

The senior lawyer also pointed out that where regulatory provisions mandate investment into a corporate structure, such structures cannot be disregarded for tax purposes by lifting the corporate veil, especially when there is no motive to avoid tax. Harish also submitted that the Hutchison corporate structure was not designed to avoid tax, and that the transaction was not a colourable device to achieve that purpose. Besides, as per Harish's contentions, the source of income lies where the transaction is affected and not where the underlying asset is situated or where the economic lies; he also said that the extraterritorial applicability of Section 195 of the Indian IT Act cannot be enforced on a non-resident without a presence in India.

The top lawyer further contended that the withholding tax provisions under Section 195 do not apply to offshore entities making offshore payments, and that the provision could be triggered only if it can be established that the payment under consideration is of a 'sum chargeable' under the IT Act. Harish contended that the findings of the tax authorities, that pursuant to the transaction the benefit of a telecom licence stood transferred to Vodafone, is misconceived, and added that there is no transfer, direct or indirect, of any licence to Vodafone, as under the telecom policy of India, a telecom licence can be held only by an Indian company.

II

MUKUL ROHATGI: AN EXTRAORDINARY JOURNEY

Born on 17 August 1955 in Mumbai

Be the change that you wish to see in the world.
—Mahatma Gandhi

Appointments to higher constitutional posts sometimes get mired in controversies. Even when Mukul Rohatgi was tipped to take over as the Attorney General of India [AG] in 2014, a letter was sent by renowned senior lawyer and politician Ram Jethmalani to Prime Minister Narendra Modi, voicing his resentment regarding Mukul's appointment.

But the negativity didn't affect Mukul one bit, though he was certainly taken aback. This letter did put on hold his appointment as AG for some time. Jethmalani had expressed his reservations, citing Mukul's weak stance against black money.

'I have asked Modiji not to appoint anybody who is opposed to the move to bring back black money from foreign accounts, to any post. It will send wrong signals . . . as one of the major reasons for the electoral victory of the BJP was the reluctance of the previous UPA government to take effective steps to bring back black money,' wrote Jethmalani. He himself had filed the case at the Supreme Court to bring back black money stashed in foreign tax havens abroad.

Mukul too wasn't very keen on being appointed India's topmost law officer. 'I was not hankering for the post. I had a great practice . . . It didn't matter beyond a point, and even if it would not have finally fructified . . . I knew it was a stumbling block, and I was confident that I would emerge victorious,' says Mukul, remembering those difficult days. 'It's indeed a great honour. Now that it has happened, I will do my best as long as I am in this post,' he says with extreme seriousness. He goes on to say that he has never opposed the move to bring back black money to India. 'This stand of Jethmalani's is mystifying and completely wrong,' he says.

The senior lawyer's diatribe against Mukul and Finance Minister, Arun Jaitley, on the issue led even Karanjawala & Co., the advocate-on-record (meaning an advocate or firm through whom one can file petitions and affidavits in the Supreme Court), to withdraw from the black-money case filed in 2009, as Raian Karanjawala is one of Mukul's closest friends.

However, people think that Mukul's handling of cases in the Supreme Court for Modi had made him a favourite choice for the coveted post, besides his friendship with Jaitley. Mukul had represented Modi and his government in the 2002 Gujarat riots cases when he was the chief minister. He had also dealt with the fake encounter deaths and the *Best Bakery* case in which Zahira Sheikh alleged that she had witnessed her family being burnt to death. Perhaps, defending such complex cases brought Mukul to the forefront and made him an obvious choice for the post. He appeared in these cases for a number of years continuously.

'Apart from being an honour, serving as the AG is one way of giving back to society or to the profession from which you have earned your name, fame, money and reputation. And these are not lifelong things—a lawyer practises for only about fifty years. I have already put in thirty-five years. If I put in forty or fifty years, out of which if I take five or ten years to give back to the profession, it's not a big deal,' says Mukul. 'I think it's a very subjective matter. Lawyers may have varying opinions about this, but for me, it's a kind of moral obligation. It has also made me aware of the challenges outside and within the legal fraternity,' he adds.

Mukul, very early in his life, had faced a series of challenges which made him train himself to confront issues peacefully and patiently. In fact, he had just emerged from a series of challenging circumstances, when he was made to confront this issue of being appointed the country's topmost law officer—something that had put his prestige at stake.

On 12 June 2014, Mukul Rohatgi was appointed the fourteenth AG of India, perhaps the youngest occupying the post so far. For him, it most definitely was a great achievement. 'I can foresee the expectations that this new post will demand of me. With a political shift, the task is indeed very daunting. My top priority as the AG would be to streamline litigation for the government in the courts,' he says.

Mukul intends to see to it that the superior courts are not flooded with frivolous and petty litigation, and that all efforts are made to check that the government does not involve itself in inter-ministerial litigation. The new post means new challenges, new responsibilities. He knows it's going to be hard, but not as hard a decision as the one he faced back in 2013.

A Tough Call

It was 2013, and Mukul was faced with perhaps one of the toughest decisions he has had to make in his life.

'Poly [Rohatgi's nickname], the doctor wants you to sign this declaration,' said Madhulika, his elder sister. She gave him a one-page document and a pen with her trembling hands.

'She could have done it herself. But I am not sure if she actually would have. I was totally shattered,' says Mukul, recounting the incident.

He took the paper and pen from his sister. There was absolutely no synchronization of what his eyes read and what his mind construed. His eyes remained riveted on the blank space where he had to sign. The tip of the pen just touched the dotted lines and he instantly withdrew his pen.

'I think I won't sign this,' Mukul told his crestfallen sister.

Nobody uttered a word. Everyone in the room looked at Mukul as he returned the unsigned document to the attendant. He, in turn, looked at Madhulika, and he knew at that moment that she had tacitly consented to his decision.

'Unless you sign this, I cannot take him off the ventilator,' said the senior doctor. Even Mukul's brother-in-law, Dr Rajiv Singla, told him that he could not just prolong his father's life by giving him artificial respiration because it ultimately meant troubling him further.

It was a tough call, but Mukul had decided not to trouble his father any more. The ventilator could have made him live for a few hours more, if not a day. It was quite a stressful moment, but Mukul had resolved not to prolong his agony. 'Certain things in life are just beyond our control. They are inevitable. One is bound by certain laws, the laws of society and the law of the land. Then, in a flash, I realized there would be no one to share or listen or exchange ideas with me,' says a still-heartbroken Mukul about his association with his father.

Mukul and his father would talk endlessly about court matters, and his father would always sum up things with his practical observations and advice. There is no one to give him that insight now.

'My father, Avadh Behari Rohatgi, was on dialysis for quite some time and had stopped going to court. I would make it a point to apprise him on a lot of cases. We would discuss them endlessly, and I would tell him about each small and big happening in the courts. This would bring a smile to his face. In these cheerful moments, he would relive his court days,' says Mukul, remembering fondly the time spent with his ailing father.

'I remember he would often tell me, "Don't give up easily . . . You must push hard and only then will the judges come around." His death shattered me completely. He had been my mentor, my guide and instructor,' says Mukul.

His father had been a lecturer at the Law Faculty in Delhi, and was a gold medallist in law from Delhi University. He was a lawyer practising in Delhi and he later became a judge of the Delhi High Court in 1972. He remained in this post till 1985. After that, till about 2010, he went back to active practice at the Supreme Court as a senior lawyer. Scores of his students have become judges of various High Courts as well as the Supreme Court of India, including two Chief Justices—the late Y.K. Sabharwal and B.N. Kirpal.

His father was fond of reading English literature, and poetry and translations of different literary works in English. He was particularly fond of Samuel Johnson's works. 'If your determination is fixed, I do not counsel you to despair. Few things are impossible to diligence and skill. Great works are performed not by strength but by perseverance,' said Samuel Johnson, a philosophy that his father was greatly inspired by.

Mukul has a wonderful library in his home, and like his father, he naturally got into reading. 'I may look more like my mother, but I have inherited my discipline and punctuality from my father. He was a disciplinarian to the core,' says Mukul.

The Background

Mukul was born in Mumbai, the business capital of India, but studied in Delhi. His childhood was quiet, and he truly enjoyed his time in school, at Modern School, Barakhamba Road, in Delhi. He was fond of playing sports and was part of the school cricket team. He also played volleyball and enjoyed swimming. He was a member of the National Cadet Corps, which encompassed institutional training conducted by the Indian military cadet corps at schools and colleges to nurture core values among Indian students, the future citizens.

'I am still in touch with my school friends, especially those who are still in Delhi. We have been in touch for the last several decades. Fashion guru Sunil Sethi; Sanjay Kapoor and his wife, Renu, who are both chartered accountants but who now follow different vocations; Navin Dang of the famous diagnostic centre in Delhi; Ravi Sachdeva of Allied Publishers; and Rohit Talwar and Ashok Minocha, who both have furniture businesses, comprise my childhood friends. None of them is in the legal profession. In fact, nobody from my batch ever came into this profession, with the exception of one person—Rajiv Nayyar, who is a senior advocate and was one batch junior to me. We are still in touch and make it a point to meet at least twice a month,' says Mukul.

However, there are several others from Modern School who have done well in the legal fraternity as well. Justice Madan B. Lokur of the Supreme Court was Mukul's senior at school. Justice Sanjay Kaul, currently the Chief Justice of the Madras High Court, and Justice Sanjeev Khanna of the Delhi High Court were both his juniors.

'I had a great time in school. We were living in Chandni Chowk, and I used to go on a cycle to Modern School. It would just take about half an hour, but in those thirty minutes, I would lose myself and enjoyed every little bit of independence,' Mukul says.

In one of those ecstatic moments he did something that he could never confess to his parents about. 'I was in class six and we had our school exams. During exam times, while riding back home, I would often recall the revision and practice exercises that the teachers would normally do before the test. The thirty-minute ride back home would also help me plan the preparation for the test. Science tests always required extra preparation,' Mukul says, recounting the incident.

It was his science test, and he had decided that he wouldn't rest or play, and would start preparing for it right after having lunch. A sincere boy, he adhered to his schedule. He finished the course well before dinner time, and did some extra bit of preparation as well. Mukul was confident that he would get full marks.

Usually, he would hum songs while cycling, but that day it was all about the three states of matter, the differences between solids, liquids and gases, etc. Talk amongst friends in school would be very different—they never discussed studies and would just indulge in regular boy-talk. Once they settled into class for the test, the boisterousness gave way to seriousness. The feeling of confidence in one's preparation, however, was short-lived. 'To my bewilderment, the test paper in front of me was that of social studies. A lesson in where, how and when things can go wrong was my analytical takeaway from this episode,' Mukul recounts with a smile on his face, remembering those largely carefree days.

He did manage to pass, and for him that incident was a real learning experience. He can never forget this—it made him realize that life itself is a test. No matter how hard one may prepare for contingencies, life has its own special ways to test each person and their calibre. It is up to individuals to cultivate habits which will help them overcome the unexpected and the unknown.

Mukul would enjoy cycling to his school, which he did from the time he entered class seven until class eleven. Traffic in those days wasn't a concern either. 'It was good exercise and gradually it developed my interest in travelling and established my love for cars. I love travelling and I love my Bentley,' says one of India's most successful lawyers.

Travelling has always been Mukul's passion. His mother was from Mumbai, a most populous city, and during vacations he along with his sister would make it a point to travel there.

The siblings had a two-point agenda in the city: to eat Alphonso mangoes and read books.

'We would often go to Kemps Corner in Mumbai, where there used to be a circulating library—the Kamal Book Library. It had a fabulous collection of books. We would pick up as many books as we could and return them in due time. My maternal uncle would clear all the bills,' says Mukul.

Mukul had inculcated the habit of reading from his father. He often picks up books at airports, and always makes it a point to write the date, year and the place of purchase inside the book. 'I have a big library in the basement of my house, and have preserved the books from my childhood days there. Even my sons are fond of reading,' he says.

Another thing that Mukul is fond of is travelling, and has already travelled to various parts of the world. Within India, he often travels to the hills and to the southern states whenever he gets an opportunity.

'Travelling to Mumbai fascinated me a lot. I was close to my maternal grandparents and would often look forward to being at their place. They had a cotton and cloth business,' he says. His grandparents used to stay at Altamount Road, which is where Antilla—billionaire industrialist Mukesh Ambani's luxury home—is located. The twenty-seven-floor Antilla is one of the tallest buildings in Mumbai. The building called Dilkusha, where Mukul's maternal grandparents lived, had been razed to give way to Antilla.

Mukul's paternal grandfather was also a cloth merchant and ran a successful business in Chandni Chowk, one of the oldest and busiest markets in Asia. The family had a palatial house in Chandni Chowk and shifted out of it only when his father became a judge in 1972.

After finishing school, Mukul studied BCom in Hansraj College, Delhi, with the idea of becoming a chartered accountant—

since it was the most sought-after profession in those days. However, he soon changed his mind to follow his father's footsteps.

But his marks couldn't fetch him a spot at the coveted Law Faculty in Delhi University. Besides, he had planned to practise in Mumbai. So he decided to relocate there instead, seeing that it was a hub of business activities. Since it was the commercial capital of India, Mumbai was the scene of a lot of commercial litigation. Mukul wanted to spend some time there and wanted to be a part of all those big corporate activities.

Journey towards Becoming a Lawyer

Mukul soon came around to accepting that he really only wanted to become a lawyer and follow his father's footsteps. He joined Government Law College in Mumbai, where he became friends with Raian Karanjawala, the founder and managing partner of Karanjawala & Co., and Anip Sachthey, now a prominent Delhi-based lawyer. Later, he became friends with Arun Jaitley and Rajiv Nayyar since they all practised together at the Delhi High Court.

Government Law College in Mumbai has produced several well-known legal personalities including the longest-serving Chief Justice of India, Yeshwant Vishnu Chandrachud, lawyers Fali Nariman and Anil Divan, and former AG Soli Sorabjee.

But after studying the law, Mukul finally realized that Delhi was the place to be. The Supreme Court, the Delhi High Court and all the tribunals were located in the capital city. Plus, it also happened to be his hometown.

Soon, it became the usual to meet friends on Saturdays for lunch at Pickwicks, a restaurant at the Claridges Hotel. 'I would regularly go out with Jaitley and Karanjawala. My father had gifted me his old Fiat car and we would all go gallivanting in it.

The day would end with me dropping them to Dhaula Kuan. From there, Jaitley would take an autorickshaw to his house in Naraina, Karanjawala would take one to Saket,' Mukul recounts.

After a year or so, his friends bought their own cars, but they all still continue to meet every Saturday for lunch. This has become a sort of ritual they have followed over twenty years.

Three People Who Influenced Him

Mukul's father, a first-generation lawyer who went on to become a judge, has been a big influence in his life. He was instrumental in inspiring him to become a lawyer. Mukul says that his senior at the Bar, the late Y.K. Sabharwal, who later became the thirty-sixth Chief Justice of India, also gave him many insights into being a good lawyer.

The third person who had a great influence on him was the principal of Modern School, the late M.N. Kapoor. 'He was a great personality and contributed a lot towards shaping my personality as well. He was tall, fair and had a striking figure. He used to speak in a very imposing manner, though softly. He knew the psychology of children and how to bring out the best in them. He paid a lot of attention to extracurricular activities and sports,' Mukul says.

The Legal Journey

In 1978, Mukul began his career with Justice Sabharwal, a prominent lawyer at the time. He was Mukul's senior for two to three years at the Delhi High Court. Mukul's father, who was a judge at that time, had requested Sabharwal to allow his son to join him. Sabharwal readily agreed. 'I owe him a lot. He gave me ample opportunities to argue his cases from day one, and this led to my popularity in court. I am grateful to him,' says Mukul.

Sabharwal was a very busy lawyer and had a lot of private and government work. His office was in a building called the Delton Cable Building, which was located at the junction of Daryaganj and Delhi Gate. The office was on the third floor and there was no lift. He had two small rooms on the terrace where the team would sit.

'If he couldn't make it to a case hearing, he would ask me to argue instead of him, rather than just take adjournments. One of the first cases I appeared in was a property dispute. In fact, it was a collusive case between the plaintiff and the defendant. There was some property transaction and they wanted some court declaration. It was a kind of mock case. My senior, the late Mr Sabharwal, appeared on one side and I appeared on the other before Justice Sultan Singh. He decided to reject the case even though there was no contest, by holding that this was discretionary relief and that he wouldn't grant any relief even if the parties had agreed,' Mukul says.

'After the matter was over, I remember Justice Sabharwal telling me that one should not feel upset because the law is what the judge said. So one should not fail to try. One should not feel let down. He taught me this mantra that you do the best for your client and move on. Because you are not the judge, you cannot judge the case. I still say the same thing to my juniors—work hard and do your best,' he says.

Many of Mukul's juniors have done rather well for themselves, including the likes of senior advocates Sandeep Sethi and Mahinder Acharya of the Delhi High Court.

1981: A Landmark Year

Two important things happened in 1981.

One, Mukul got married. His wife, Vasudha, comes from a family of lawyers. Her father, the late G.L. Sanghi, was a senior lawyer, and her grandfather was a lawyer in Nagpur. She also studied the law herself. But she gave up her practice after the couple's first child, Nikhil, was born. It was her decision. Both their sons are now lawyers.

In 1981, Mukul also started his independent practice. 'I would do all sorts of cases. I got first-hand experience in handling property and family disputes, besides intellectual property cases. I also dealt with a lot of corporate and criminal cases at the Delhi High Court. I think it was because of this varied experience that I got noticed and got due recognition,' he says.

Mukul experienced a period of struggle in the initial years, and then one day something unusual happened, which gave Mukul an insight, helping him emerge from this struggle. His friend Arun Jaitley received a call late at night asking him to take on the position of the Additional Solicitor General (ASG) of India. The then prime minister, V.P. Singh, had called up Jaitley to take over this coveted post. In fact, all of Jaitley's friends, including Mukul, were waiting for him at the Claridges Hotel till late in the night when Jaitley had gone for his meeting.

It was then that Mukul realized that Jaitley was not a designated senior lawyer. 'I decided to help him get the designation. In those days, the Delhi High Court was a small place, with just twelve to fifteen judges. I, therefore, took up the issue and walked into the chambers of the judges, especially Justices B.N. Kirpal and Sunanda Bhandare. I met them during lunchtime and requested them to meet on the same day and designate Jaitley as a senior lawyer,' reveals Mukul.

The judges were kind enough to honour his request and, to Mukul's utter surprise, 'The judges designated my dear friend as a senior advocate at four in the afternoon. The rules were different those days and the procedures were simpler.'

As a Senior

Mukul was himself designated as a senior lawyer in 1993 by the Delhi High Court. His practice flourished till 1999, when he shifted to the Supreme Court after his appointment as the ASG. It was a difficult decision to shift to a new setting, though he visited the apex court frequently.

'It was like going into a different arena and meeting a different set of lawyers and, above all, arguing before judges who had different outlooks and perspectives. In summary, it was like getting out of your comfort zone. It had nothing to do with money,' Mukul says in retrospect.

There were many juniors who had become judges by then. However, Mukul had no apprehension or inhibition in dealing with juniors turned judges. 'I feel it is a process of evolution; young people will get older, and older people will get still more mature. A lawyer with thirty to forty years of experience, when s/he addressing the court, is not the same person who is sitting there—it is the institution that you have to see. Lawyers and judges will come and go. So you address the court ultimately,' he says.

When he started appearing at the Supreme Court, the judges would always encourage the youngsters. 'One of my first reported cases in the Supreme Court was in 1985, concerning the Natraj Cinema Complex. The bench comprised Justices Chinnappa Reddy and K. Jagannatha Shetty. It was a case relating to the sale of the cinema hall. We lost in the first court and the first appeal; the client couldn't afford to pay the fees of the senior lawyer. So Sabharwal asked me to argue. I argued the case, and we succeeded at the Supreme Court. That client, in turn, got me lots of other clients, since he could not pay me much then,' Mukul says with a smile.

The Turning Point

It was in 1999 that Mukul was appointed as the ASG in the Atal Behari Vajpayee–led government. 'It was an honour to serve as the Additional Solicitor General, but I must say that it was an extremely difficult job. It was a learning experience and an insight into how the government works and how litigation is handled. It took me almost two years to get a good grasp of it,' he says, remembering those days.

Mukul considers his shift to the Supreme Court extremely significant and challenging. 'I guess this was a turning point. I had a great practice at the High Court, but I typically only did cases from Delhi. It was only when I shifted to the Supreme Court that I could enjoy a pan-India experience,' he says.

It was as ASG that he got an insight into how the bureaucracy actually worked. 'I found that the bureaucrats were only shuffling papers around. There was no one who would ever make a clear decision. In many cases, I had to take the final call. I discovered that the system was very slow,' he remarks.

The real turning point in his life was leaving the Delhi High Court and then doing cases on a larger canvas by working for the government and various PSUs, be it the 2G spectrum case, the coal scam, mining matters at the Special Forest Bench for Goa, Karnataka and Orissa, or cases of petrol pump cancellations. There were cases that would attract public attention, whether it meant appearing for yoga guru Baba Ramdev, or attending to complaints against Maharashtra politician Raj Thackeray—and that made all the difference.

In 2004, the government changed and Mukul had to resume private practice at the Supreme Court. He had to make a tough decision whether to go back to the Delhi High Court or continue at the apex court. But Mukul decided to stick on in the Supreme Court and not go back to the High Court, where he was comfortable. His practice at the Supreme Court gradually developed. 'The number of cases that I argue every day shows the trust that litigants bestow on me. I would hear my name being mentioned and people saying "That's Mukul Rohatgi!" in the corridors. This usually happens on Mondays and Fridays, when miscellaneous matters are taken up. One can find me rushing from one courtroom to another,' he says.

Information is exchanged when people discuss how Mukul handles a wide spectrum of matters which include both civil and criminal cases. This is the common type of 'corridor talk' that one gets to hear at the apex court.

'There are some successful cases that have become quite memorable for me now. One of them relates to the constitutional issue of a floor test in the Jharkhand Assembly, which the then governor, Syed Sibtey Razi, was reluctant to order in March 2005. I succeeded in impressing upon the Supreme Court to direct the then pro-tem Speaker of the Jharkhand Legislative Assembly, Pradeep Kumar Balmuchu, to conduct a composite floor test in the assembly to ascertain who enjoyed the majority—the then chief minister, Shibu Soren, appointed by governor Syed Sibtey Razi, or former chief minister Arjun Munda,' he says.

Mukul appeared for Munda and argued that the governor had already given a long time to Soren to prove his majority in the house and that this could lead to horse-trading. Besides, Razi had 'murdered' the constitutional conventions of inviting the single-largest party or engaging in the pre-poll alliance to form the government by asking the Jharkhand Mukti Morcha (JMM)–Congress alliance (which had a combined strength of twenty-six), to form the government despite the NDA having thirty-six seats.

The Supreme Court gave Mukul an opportunity to appear in big matters. One such high-profile case that made the headlines was the high-voltage legal battle between the Ambani siblings—Mukesh and Anil—over natural gas. After a bitter public battle over the division of the Reliance empire, less than two years after the Ambani family patriarch Dhirubhai's death, Mukesh and Anil reached a family settlement spelt out by their mother, Kokilaben, in June 2005. As per the settlement, the energy and petrochemicals business went to Mukesh, and the power, financial services and telecom business was given to Anil. However, the bitterness between the two brothers did not cease.

The Anil Ambani group firm, Reliance Natural Resources Ltd (RNRL), moved the Bombay High Court, seeking the supply of 28 million cubic metres of natural gas per day at a price of $2.34 per MMBtu, a price that was 44 per cent lower than the government-approved rate of $4.20 per MMBtu, for seventeen years from the D6 field in the Krishna–Godavari basin (KG-D6) operated by the Mukesh–led Reliance Industries Limited (RIL) for RNRL's proposed 7800 MW power plant in Dadri, Uttar Pradesh. The Bombay High Court directed RIL to reach an amicable agreement with RNRL for the gas supply as per the family memorandum of understanding (MoU) signed in June 2005. While RNRL got a favourable verdict from the High Court, the Supreme Court dealt a severe blow to the younger brother, Anil, ruling that the government had the last word on the pricing and utilization of national assets. The Supreme Court headed by then Chief Justice of India, K.G. Balakrishnan, upheld the government's sovereign right to pricing and utilization of scarce natural resources and also said that the Ambani family MoU dividing the gas was not binding on the ground that 3 million shareholders of RIL–RNRL did not know its contents. 'While I, along with senior lawyer Ram Jethmalani, represented Anil Ambani both at the High Court and the Supreme Court, I had senior lawyers Harish Salve, Abhishek Manu Singhvi and Rohinton Nariman as my opponents in court, as they had been enlisted by Mukesh Ambani,' he says, recounting the case that resulted in the landmark Supreme Court judgement that deemed all natural resources as public assets, which no private or public company could lay claim to.

Mukul also represented the Italian Embassy, when two Italian marines were accused of shooting two Indian fishermen in 2012, off the coast of Kerala, thereby stoking political tensions between the two countries. The Supreme Court recently allowed one of the marines to go home for medical treatment if he promised to return to India. The co-accused Italian marine is currently out on bail and residing at the Italian Embassy in New Delhi. 'While I, on behalf of Italy, argued that the incident happened in international waters and that the marines should face trial in Rome, India disagreed, saying that the matter should be handled by its own courts,' he says. The marines have been charged under anti-piracy legislation.

Mukul has also defended Varun Gandhi, an estranged member of the Nehru–Gandhi political clan, who was accused of inciting religious hatred during election campaigning in 2009. He was arrested under the stringent National Security Act, 1980, by the Uttar Pradesh government. The Supreme Court later ordered the charges to be dropped against the young leader.

Mukul also counts current Tamil Nadu chief minister, Jayalalithaa, amongst his clients, having defended her in corruption cases. 'I have argued on behalf of the Gujarat government in matters concerning the riots that took place in the state. I have also been representing the accused in the Commonwealth Games scam and the 2G Scam. I have also appeared for several high-profile accused and big corporates, like Essar in the alleged 2G spectrum illegal allotment case, in which former telecom minister, A. Raja, is the prime accused, and Dravida Munnetra Kazhagam (DMK) chief, M. Karunanidhi's daughter Kanimozhi, also a former minister, is one of the co-accused facing trial,' Mukul says, recounting the several feathers in his cap.

After assuming the office of the AG, he has now recused himself from all these cases, citing conflict of interest.

An Unusual Case

It was an unusual case, a case of conscience, and Mukul took it up because of his concern for humanity. 'I call it unusual because the client didn't come to me; I approached the court to do the case for this person. He was a labourer,' Mukul says.

'Had my father been alive, he would have certainly appreciated my decision. Not that he was a great thinker, but his thinking, to a great extent, was influenced by Samuel Johnson and his writings. And in this particular context, he would have loved to recall Johnson: "The true measure of a man is how he treats someone who can do him absolutely no good,"' Mukul says.

In this particular case, Mukul had no expectations from his client. It all started when he was watching a reality show. 'Who would do such a case? Is there any lawyer who would ever think of doing such a case,' said the TV anchor to his viewers. Mukul was participating in this TV show and he decided to go ahead with it.

In summary, the matter revolved around a case of mistaken identity. One of the labourers in a construction company had the same name as his contractor. Now, this contractor had committed a crime, but the labourer had been caught instead and was even being tried for the offence; he consequently remained in jail for a number of years.

'I got a writ petition filed at the Supreme Court. I took up the matter pro bono and argued before a bench of Justices P. Sathasivam and J. Chelameswar that this was a case of gross miscarriage of justice coupled with a blatant violation of the right to life guaranteed under Article 21 of the Constitution—which required the court to take urgent corrective steps,' says Mukul. Finally, the Supreme Court ordered an inquiry into the case; the result was in favour of the labourer and he was subsequently released.

Mukul says, 'I felt happy doing it. "Happiness is when what you think, what you say and what you do are in harmony," says Mahatma Gandhi, the Father of our Nation.' Mukul continues, 'In life, it's all about taking the initiative. It was a genuine case, a genuine cause and I had genuine concern—and the outcome was positive. Such kinds of cases and incidents bring immense happiness.'

In the courtroom, it's all business for Mukul. People have often accused him of being too belligerent and rude. But when he is in court, representing his client, he ensures that his voice is heard even if it is at the cost of flailing his arms and shouting down his opponent. However, these criticisms of his attitude don't really impact Mukul. 'This is the normal way I argue. It is never meant to offend anyone. I am polite inside and outside the courts. I feel it is important for a lawyer to adhere to professional ethics. I firmly believe in honesty. To never compromise your position or the position of your client is something I would always advise to all would-be lawyers. You cannot talk behind the client's back. You cannot think of doing anything which will harm the interest of the client,' he says.

Journey from ASG to AG

It has been a decade-long journey. Mukul has had a gap of ten years from 2004 till now. He had a good stint as a lawyer with a private practice. He is a hard worker and doesn't like to keep things pending, whether the matter concerns a lawyer, a minister or a bureaucrat. Mukul works seven days a week and has been doing so all his life.

'If one has to work twice the number of hours, then one should be ready for it. This is the message that I see has gone down during the present Narendra Modi–led government. I find that bureaucrats, ministers, seniors, juniors, all are working at a furious pace, seven days a week. I meet government officers at all times. I haven't met any officer till date who has said that he is not available on a Saturday or Sunday. So there is only one mantra: Work, work and work,' he says.

The volume of work that Mukul tackles is tremendous—there are thirty-eight ministries, but only one AG. 'A lot of people today feel that lawyers don't enjoy a very good name in society. One way to redeem this image is to do some work for society, some free work, some pro bono cases,' he says.

In 1993, India opened up to the world, and the wave of liberalization ushered in many advantages as well as disadvantages. It also paved the way for international disputes and foreign arbitration. Litigation has changed over a period of time, and now is the time for specialization. Now, one comes across things like electricity litigation, information technology litigation, competition law, mines litigation, apart from the sheer number of tribunals that populate the legal space.

Opportunities today are much greater because of these tribunals; when Mukul started out, there was only one tribunal. 'Survival skills have now acquired great significance. Lawyers need to have a strong sense of professional ethics. They must have respect for the court. They should be honest with the court even if it means that your client will lose the case,' he says.

Mukul believes that lawyers have to be constantly vigilant to see how the bench is reacting. They should possess the tact to present their point, be brief and also have a strong sense of indulging in relevant and appropriate paperwork. They should be able to think on their feet and should be able to diffuse the tense atmosphere prevailing in a courtroom by resorting to humour, if and when required. It is certainly a tall order and certainly challenging.

'I work hard and make all efforts to make my argument heavy and meaningful; my focus is always to go straight to the point and deliver my arguments in such a manner that my principal argument or arguments counter all counterarguments. Tone is an accompaniment. Every lawyer has a strategy, a way of doing things. The important thing, however, is to maintain the decorum and one's code of practice,' Mukul says; his words can be a mantra for the young breed of lawyers who are just starting their careers. 'Presenting a reasonable and practical solution goes a long way in court,' he says.

Mukul is of the opinion that the cognitive processing and element of subjectivity play a significant role in the interpretation of what a lawyer intends to convey through his arguments in a case. This element of variability and individual expertise of judges (who come from different High Courts, with diverse experiences and backgrounds) may play an important role in how a case has to be argued and how it will be easily understood by two or three judges sitting on a particular bench. 'You have to keep in view that one judge may not know the intricacies of a business law as s/he may have expertise in other laws like criminal matters and may take time to understand a particular business matter. You must address that judge with the same dignity and respect even if he is not so familiar with the concerned subject. And it would be appropriate to take him through the basics, which the other judge may be too well versed with,' he says.

Mukul is also of the opinion that the judiciary taking too long to decide on a case is a matter of concern, and believes in the adage that justice delayed is very often justice denied. 'No government ever thought that dispensation of justice, or the judiciary, was as important as other things like agriculture or finance, so by default the law received step-motherly treatment. These things are quite disturbing. I think one needs to have the strength and courage to get things rolling towards a better and brighter future, and what is ultimately required is a sense of discipline,' he says.

'Mukul sir is a towering figure with an equally magnanimous heart and robust energy. He is a master craftsman at handling the court, be it complex legal matters or a short, simple one,' says D.L. Chidananda, a Delhi lawyer who admires Mukul a lot.

A typical day in Mukul's life begins at 6.30 a.m. He is in court by 10.15 a.m. Then at 4 p.m., he goes to his office and finishes all the work on his table by 8.30 p.m. 'I do a lot of cases. I generally don't turn away people. I have never done that. I am quite happy and satisfied. I have had a good life, a good career, a good family and, I would say, a good reputation. And I would not want to be anybody else or anything else in terms of my profession,' he says.

What He Likes Most

Mukul loves his morning walks and tries never to miss a single day. He is fond of swimming as well and, time permitting, goes for a swim whenever he can. While he isn't religious in a traditional, ritualistic way, he does believe in God. 'I have a small mandir at home, and I do my prayers for two to three minutes in the morning. I neither believe in auspicious and inauspicious days, nor in palmistry and astrology. But I prefer to give to charity, which I feel is better than giving money to pandits,' he says.

He is a regular contributor to the Blind Relief Association, HelpAge India and to an orphanage in East of Kailash, New Delhi. On an average, he donates around Rs 20 lakh a year, especially on occasions like his father's and mother's death anniversaries and on the festival of Diwali too.

Hall of Legal Fame

Mukul Rohatgi is the fourteenth—present—Attorney General of India. He is a senior advocate at the Supreme Court and has also served as the ASG.

His forceful presentation of facts in a modulating tone, accompanied by gestures, especially that of spreading his arms wide, has made him a unique figure and a force to reckon with. His clients comprise the rich and famous. On an 'admission' day at court, one can feel the presence of his energy shuffling from one courtroom to another through the busy and crowded corridors, trying to attend to scores of cases.

Mukul has a very balanced approach. He never loses his temper and is even-handed with everyone. His client-friendly and result-oriented approach is greatly appreciated. Even if there is nothing in a case, he will try to push his efforts to the maximum. He never gives up a case halfway and does his best to take it to its logical conclusion. He enjoys being in court and enjoys talking to people.

Mukul is easy to brief and is very approachable. You just have to brief him for ten minutes and he will be able to gauge the peculiarities of a case and know what to put across to the court. He has good court-craft. He articulates his point in a simple way and hammers it home. He may have a forceful way of arguing, but he remains polite. 'He has the great ability to relate to people and skilfully handle his clients,' says Mukul's friend, Raian Karanjawala, who engaged him as a senior counsel in most of his cases before Mukul became the AG in 2014. He feels Mukul's own work got affected after he chose to take up the constitutional post. 'Mukul is extremely sociable and continues to attend all family functions and get-togethers with his friends,' Karanjawala says.

'Working with Mr Rohatgi is a continuous education—especially regarding how to break down complex questions of fact and law and presenting it in a simple, appealing way to the court,' says Abhinav Mukerji, a young lawyer who often assists Mukul in important matters.

Rohatgi's sister, Madhulika, who lives in Delhi, feels that her brother, Poly, remains cool and unruffled under pressure. 'Work makes him feel good. He doesn't ever appear hassled. He is fearless, forthright, spontaneous, very generous, and is very protective of me. I can depend on him, and this is a big reassurance for me since my parents are no more. When I look at my brother, an image of a duck comes to my mind. Ducks appear cool and calm and unruffled on the surface, but paddle furiously underneath,' says Madhulika.

THE CASE

Manohar Lal Sharma v. The Principal Secretary [(2014) 9 SCC 516]

Judgement delivered by bench comprising Chief Justice R.M. Lodha, and Justices Madan B. Lokur and Kurian Joseph.

Case Details

Two PILs were filed in 2012 by advocate M.L. Sharma and Common Cause, a Delhi-based NGO working on corruption issues, represented by activist lawyer Prashant Bhushan. The PILs prayed for the cancellation of all coal blocks allotted to private companies since 1993 as well as a thorough probe into the allocations by an independent agency. They accused the government of granting largesse to the private companies.

The Supreme Court finally cancelled 204 of 218 coal-block allocations after declaring them illegal, arbitrary and against public interest. These allocations of coal blocks were made during the thirty-six meetings of the screening committee and through the government dispensation route during the previous NDA and UPA regimes from 1993–2009. The apex court, which examined the allocations made to mining companies for their captive use in the pre-auction era till 2010, had ruled that the allocations had been done in an illegal manner by adopting an 'ad hoc and casual' approach 'without application of mind', and 'common good and public interest have, thus, suffered heavily' due to lack of fair and transparent procedure, resulting ultimately in 'unfair distribution' of 'national wealth'.

However, the apex court allowed two coal blocks (Moher and Moher–Amroli Extension) allotted to Sasan Power Ultra Mega Power Projects, operated by Reliance Power Ltd, and also allowed one each given to the central government PSU, National Thermal Power Corporation (NTPC) (the Pakri Barwadih coal block) and SAIL (the Tasra coal block) to continue to operate as the benefit of the coal blocks was passed on to the public.

While doing so, the Supreme Court acted on the Narendra Modi–led NDA government's assurance that it was fully prepared to face the cancellations and go ahead with the auctioning of the natural resource. But it rejected the government's request to save forty functional coal blocks and six ready-to-function ones. It allowed forty-two functional coal blocks to operate for six months, provided they paid an additional levy of Rs 295 per metric tonne of coal extracted to make up for the loss as per the national auditor's report. Another reason for allowing them to continue operations for a while was to give the government breathing space to manage the emerging situation.

At present, the CBI is investigating the case. The Supreme Court also appointed additional sessions judge, Bharat Parashar, to preside over the special CBI court set up exclusively to hold day-to-day trials in cases related to the coal block allocation scam. Chandigarh-based senior advocate R.S. Cheema has been appointed as the special public prosecutor to assist the special court.

The three affected industry bodies—the Coal Producers Association, the Independent Power Producers Association of India and the Sponge Iron Manufacturers Association—painted a grim picture, saying that cancellation would have an adverse impact on the country's economy and would result in a severe power crisis. Besides, any order of the apex court should have a prospective effect and all the allocations should be examined on a case-to-case basis.

It was submitted that: government companies were not in a position to supply the required quantity of coal; power stations have a supply of less than one week of coal and, therefore, there are possibilities of power outages; as many as ten power plants belonging to NTPC and Damodar Valley Corporation have been shut down because of shortage of coal supply by Coal India Ltd (CIL); there is an issue of poor quality of coal supplied by CIL; huge investments up to about Rs 2.87 lakh crore have been made in 157 coal blocks as on December 2012; investments in end-use plants have been made to the extent of about Rs 4 lakh crore; the employment of almost 10 lakh people is at stake; end-use plants would become redundant; loans to the extent of about Rs 2.5 lakh crore given by banks and financial institutions would become non-performing assets; the State Bank of India may suffer a loss of up to Rs 78,263 crore, which is almost 7.9 per cent of its net worth for 2013; other public sector banks such as the Punjab National Bank and the Union Bank will receive a massive setback; and the country's dependence on coal as a primary fuel source with up to 60 per cent for power generation may result in inflationary trends.

Private miners further contended that cancellation of the blocks would hit investors' confidence, cause acute distress in some industries, affect 28,000 MW of power capacity, while the closure of coal mines would cause an estimated loss of Rs 4.4 lakh crore in terms of royalty, cess, direct and indirect taxes, besides raising the cost of coal imports even more in 2016–17 to the extent of Rs 1.44 lakh crores (without de-allocation) and setting back the process of extraction and effective utilization of coal by eight years.

Impact
The coal scam is the mother all scandals in India. An astonishing amount of close to Rs 2 lakh crore is believed to have been squandered away on account of this. The amount, though gigantic in proportion, was not the only factor that mattered. The impact of the Supreme Court cancelling the allotments was profound and multidimensional.

India is a mineral-rich country. Its future and prosperity with regard to energy are crucially dependent on mining and using its most abundant, affordable and dependant energy supply—coal. It is no exaggeration to say that coal is regarded by many as the 'black diamond'. The country's coal reserves are mostly spread across seven states: Maharashtra, Madhya Pradesh, Chhattisgarh, Orissa, Jharkhand, Andhra Pradesh and West Bengal.

The energy sector was arguably the most affected, for many of the running and upcoming power plants are coal-fired. Now that their captive mine allocations stand cancelled, power producers stared at ambiguity and uncertainty. And at stake were thousands of crores of rupees—at least corporates and industry bodies claimed so.

Some estimates said that a short supply of coal will put as many as twelve major power projects that envisage an investment of Rs 36,000 crore for a projected generation capacity of 7230 MW in jeopardy.

The banking system, already reeling under massive non-performing assets, received a rude shock. Banks have already lent crores of rupees with coal blocks as collateral. Here at one stroke, collaterals have vanished. Banks are believed to have lent Rs 5 lakh crore to the power sector alone in this manner. The banking industry feels that even interest payment on these loans would be difficult for some companies after this manner of cancellation of mines has been effected.

But such economic implications alone cannot determine a case.

With the allocation of 204 captive mines out of 214 cancelled, one obvious consequence was higher imports—a situation which will have trickle-down effects till the end on a power consumer. Higher imports would mean a higher cost of production and, hence, higher tariff. Moreover, there is already a demand–supply mismatch. In 2014, for example, India imported 171 million tonnes of coal at $16.41 billion. In the previous year, inbound shipments stood at 145 million tonnes ($17.01 billion), say analysts. According to some estimates, the coal import bill in 2016 is likely to widen by $6.22 billion. Experts point out that a higher import bill would also have a bearing on the country's current account deficit too.

One common impact of the 2G spectrum scam and the coal scandal is that both led to competitive bidding for natural resources. Though experts are divided on the benefits of the auction of scarce resources, the process, it seems, is here to stay for a long time to come.

Though a higher spectrum price in the auction may not have resulted in a steep hike in mobile tariff, coal is a different story. One need not long for the story of costlier coal to unveil as the auction process in under way. Unlike the telecom story, where even state-owned companies had to bid for spectrum, in the coal segment, PSUs don't need to participate in the auction. The private sector would pitch for a level-playing field.

On the political front, the verdict came as the last nail on the coffin of the UPA II government. For former prime minister Manmohan Singh, his reputation was blown to smithereens. Singh was in charge of the coal ministry in the UPA II regime, which allocated mines through screening committees. The media had reported that the CBI probing the scam reached his doorsteps too.

In a nutshell, with this verdict of the apex court, the so-called coal rush came crashing down. The verdict underscored the charges of crony capitalism. The power, steel and cement sectors started bracing for an overhaul. Corporates were forced to redraw their business strategies. Coming close on the heels of verdicts on a series of scandals, the Supreme Court judgement on the coal scam spurred a new thinking in political and corporate establishments. The old ways won't work any more. A fresh beginning in the government–corporate relation has dawned. Hopefully, this chapter is without blemishes. That is the biggest impact.

Winning Strokes

AG Mukul Rohatgi argued that the central government was fully prepared to take things forward by conducting auctions in a time-bound manner.

He stated that all the apprehensions put forward by the private sector, including the economic implications or fallout of the cancellation of coal block allotments and the possible adverse impact that it may have on other socio-economic factors, have been taken into consideration and that the Centre is fully prepared to face the consequences of the cancellation of all coal blocks, if need be, and is desirous of moving forward.

Expounding on the alternative consequence, he said that CIL, a PSU, can take over and continue the extraction of coal from the forty-four coal blocks without adversely affecting the rights of those employed in them. And even if the allotment of these forty-four coal blocks is cancelled, the central government can ensure that coal production will not stop.

Rohatgi, the top law officer of the country, submitted that all the allottees of coal blocks should be directed to pay an additional levy of Rs 295 per metric tonne of coal extracted from the date of extraction to make good the loss according to the Comptroller and Auditor General's report on the coal scam. In the case of allottees supplying coal to the power sector, they should be mandated to enter into Power Purchase Agreements (PPAs) with the state utility or distribution company, so that the benefit is passed on to the consumers.

Opposing the setting up of a court-appointed committee to consider each individual case to determine whether the coal block allotments should be cancelled or not, Mukul said that the process of allotment cannot be reopened collaterally through the appointment of a committee. He said that this would virtually amount to nullifying the judgement, and that the beneficiaries of the flawed process must suffer the consequences thereof, and that the appointment of a committee would really amount to permitting a body to examine the correctness of the judgement, which is clearly impermissible.

III

ABHISHEK MANU SINGHVI: RISING ABOVE CHALLENGES

Born on 24 February 1959 in Jodhpur

Courage in adversity, patience in prosperity, oratory in assembly,
bravery in battle, modesty in fame, attachment to knowledge . . .
We can only try.
—Unknown

HE WAS on top of the world!

Takdi ko vote do!

Takdi ko vote do!

He would climb on to an elder's shoulders, shouting slogans, feeling on top of the world from his cosy vantage point. It was fun holding the megaphone, and when the other voices would fade, he would take over and shout at the top of his voice, *'Takdi ko vote do!'* His right fist closed, he would involuntarily raise it in the air while chanting.

Barely three and a half years old, he could hardly understand what the slogan meant. He would just echo what the others said. The year was 1962. There was a lot of excitement in the frenzied crowd. And among the crowd, little Abhishek Manu Singhvi— today, a stalwart politician and renowned lawyer—would fancy himself a great orator.

'It's been more than fifty years now, but the feeling still reverberates in me. This election campaign took place in Jodhpur. In those days, they used to have hand-megaphone campaigns. My house was just opposite Sojati Gate in Jodhpur, which separates the old city from the new city. It was from here that the campaigning would start,' Singhvi says, remembering those heady, carefree days.

'Takdi' in Rajasthani means 'the scales of justice'. Singhvi's father, Dr L.M. Singhvi, stood as an independent candidate from Jodhpur in the 1962 Lok Sabha elections, and the takdi was his symbol. Dr Singhvi, Abhishek's father, had just returned to India from Harvard and was not even thirty years old when he stood for and won the elections; he was already a well-known figure in his twenties. He was a gold medallist from Allahabad University, known as the Oxford of the East. He completed his LLB degree from Jaipur, and was the first person from Rajasthan to be awarded the Rotary Scholarship to Harvard in 1954. He received his PhD from Cornell in 1956 and became an assistant professor at Berkeley.

It was Kanhaiyalal Munshi, lawyer and founder of Bharatiya Vidya Bhavan, on whose advice Dr Singhvi moved to Jodhpur in 1957, otherwise he would have settled in Delhi. And in just four years, at the age of twenty-nine, he had become one of the top law practitioners in the Rajasthan High Court. Abhishek's grandfather, D.M. Singhvi, was a Congress Party member all his life. He died in 1957. Had he been alive, he would have contested the 1962 elections himself. However, that year, it was Abhishek's father who was almost chosen to contest the elections on a Congress Party ticket. Unfortunately, before the election, some of Abhishek's grandfather's so-called political 'friends' conspired against his father to oust him from the party ticket.

'This sabotage and subterfuge against my father was the last straw, and he decided to stand on his own, as an independent candidate, against the official Congress Party candidate, Mr N.K. Sanghi of Sanghi Motors—one of the richest men in Rajasthan. Nobody expected my father to win. But it was my father's idealism and a good amount of support from the youth that made him win the elections,' Abhishek says. The entire campaign cost around Rs 15,000!

Abhishek remained in Jodhpur till his fourth birthday, and has vivid memories of his hometown. 'I had a lovely childhood. We lived in a flat on the first floor. It was in the heart of the city, next to the famous Minerva Building and Minerva Cinema. The people around were warm, genuine, helpful and cordial,' he says.

Abhishek was a naughty child and had a nasty habit of picking up certain objects, especially expensive utensils or other shiny things, running to the balcony and then throwing them down in the crowded marketplace at the passers-by below. Someone or the other would fetch the articles back and, on occasion, the shopkeepers below would uncomplainingly do so.

Far from being scolded or reprimanded, Abhishek was often pampered and treated like a little god. 'I don't know if it was to do with gender monopoly then. I happened to be the only male child in the families of my father and his two brothers—the only male child amongst seven girls! I was loved to a fault by my grandmother and aunts. My grandmother doted on me. If my mother, the only one to ever scold me, did so, she immediately earned the strong disapproval and ire of all the elders in the house. I was thoroughly pampered, and I enjoyed every bit of it, perhaps justifiably, because the Singhvi clan would have suffered extinction if it hadn't been for me!' says Abhishek with a chuckle and a twinkle in his eye.

The Background

Abhishek would mostly have continued to live in Jodhpur had it not been for the 1962 elections. After his father won the elections, the family relocated to Delhi. The family stayed in South Avenue and later shifted to 19 Janpath, next to where the present-day Le Meridian hotel is located. Barely 2 kilometres from their Janpath home was the school he was admitted to: St Columba's

School. 'I am a loyal Columban. My most glorious period was at
Columba's. Academically, I was a bright student, a top ranker,
and St Columba's was academically numero uno in India for
several decades till the early 1980s. In class nine, I was awarded the
Lovi Chandrashekhar Prize, which was given to the top-ranking
student amongst all five sections of the batch,' Singhvi says. He
went on to top all sections in class ten as well and was awarded the
Santosh Memorial Prize.

Abhishek continued his stellar academic performance and
emerged as the top-rank holder in the entire country in his school-
leaving Senior Cambridge examinations. He got five points with
four 95 per cents and one 90 per cent, ranking him first in India,
with a 94 per cent average. All top Indian schools then followed
the Senior Cambridge system, but the famous ones—Doon,
Mayo, St Edwards, etc.—barely had one five-pointer every two
or three years. 'Our 1975 batch had ten five-pointers from our
school alone—a feat that hasn't yet been equalled by any school
(including ours) since its inception in the 1930s or thereafter!'
says Abhishek proudly.

Abhishek was a very bright and studious child, but serious,
introverted and shy. 'I was taught and groomed by three Irish
brothers, Corbett, Morrisey and Foley, and one class teacher, Mr
C.I. Jose, the latter remaining with us from class eight to eleven.
I owe a lot to them. I was chosen for all the important speeches,
elocutions, declamations. I was good at speaking, but typical of
an introvert, was never confident. I was always overly self-critical.
Even today I am a complete introvert, virtually an anti-social, but
I still have a public face. I don't like to go to parties unless I am
forced to. I love to be by myself, love to read, or sit and watch TV,
or merely chat with a few close school friends,' he reveals.

Abhishek still keeps in touch with his school friends. 'Whenever
I am tired or want to put my feet up, my two friends from Delhi

come over or vice versa. We go to the movies together on Friday evenings. They are better friends with my wife, more than any of her girlfriends, since she came to Delhi as a young eighteen-year-old.'

After school, Abhishek chose to pursue a degree in economics at one of the most reputed colleges in the country, St Stephen's College. Many present High Court judges, potential future Chief Justices of India and eminent business heads were not only his college batchmates but classmates as well. These include the Chief Justice of the Allahabad High Court, Dhananjaya Chandrachud; the Chief Justice of the Madras High Court, Sanjay Kaul; Feedback Infra Private Ltd chairman, Vinayak Chatterjee; worldwide president and CEO of MasterCard, Ajay Banga; Chief Economic Adviser to the Indian government, Arvind Subramanian; worldwide chief executive of Diageo, Ivan Menezes; ambassador of India to the European Union, Belgium and Luxembourg, Manjeev Singh Puri; Additional Secretary, Ministry of Rural Development, K.P. Krishnan, and many more. 'The batch,' he says, 'to put it mildly, has not done too badly.'

Becoming a Lawyer

Abhishek's father was a busy man, but was very warm towards kids. He never forced his children into doing anything. Abhishek chose the law as his profession through a process of elimination. 'It probably happened because the ambience was all law. I could see law, I could smell law, and everything had the flavour of law at home,' he says. 'Like my father, I have never forced anything on my children. My sons are both lawyers. But my elder son is not practising. He is into business and consultancy and is settled abroad. My younger son was working with senior lawyer Shyam Diwan, an outstanding lawyer, but more importantly, a great human being. He is now with Agarwal Associates. My wife, and my younger sister, Abhilasha, have both done law, but are not at all interested in it,' he continues.

Abhishek's legal career is much shorter than what people think. He studied law at Trinity College (University of Cambridge) in the UK. He enrolled in 1981, but effectively started practising in 1985–86, after completing his PhD. At the beginning of his legal career, he started out with his father, but left for Cambridge in 1981 to pursue his doctorate under the legendary Sir William Wade. He was in Cambridge from 1982–84. 'My father never wanted me to do a PhD and was keen that I should start practising. But I managed to do my PhD from Cambridge because of my mother, who supported me throughout. Getting a PhD means ploughing a very lonely furrow. There is hardly any supervision. The success rate for Cambridge PhDs is abysmal. Less than 50 per cent of those who start it end up completing it. Those who do complete it, do so in an average of six years. One faces constant insecurity, and the urge to go out into the real world and start earning is strong. Several years of work can be rejected in one viva voce of three to four hours and set you back by instalments of one year's duration each time! I was lucky enough to complete my degree in three years and be approved,' he says.

One of Abhishek's abiding regrets is that despite the insistence of the top Indian law publisher in those days, N.M. Tripathi & Co., who persuaded him for over two years to rewrite parts of his thesis before it could be sent for publication, that never happened. After returning to India, he rapidly became busier and busier with each passing day. The thesis never got published, only because Abhishek had insisted on doing it himself. It would have been the first of its kind, a comprehensive comparative study of emergency powers vis-à-vis the US, the UK, India and international treaty law. It ran into 1,00,000 words, with a second volume of equal length, comprising only footnotes. Even now, very few books on the subject have been published, and none with a comparative perspective. 'Contrary to my professor's advice, I allowed the perfect to be the enemy of the good,' says Abhishek regretfully.

In the Rajasthani community, getting a scholarship and going abroad was considered to be a big achievement then, and people recognized Abhishek for it. 'We used to have annual lectures in my grandfather D.M. Singhvi's memory. On these occasions, I would generally carry out the responsibility of an emcee and also be a speaker myself,' he says.

Life was taking its own course pursuant to his return to India, when he got a very unusual case to handle. 'My mother, Kamla Singhvi, got a file and asked me to take up the case. Perhaps it was coming from her social circle or a distant relative requesting some kind of an opinion. My father had seen the file and told my mother to seek my opinion on this matter,' Abhishek remembers. Abhishek looked at the unusually small-sized file that carried hardly any papers and was quite unlike a legal document.

'My mother had made a file of photographs of girls whom she had seen as prospective brides for me, complete with biodata and photographs. At the top of the pile was Anita. I was in Jodhpur for a lecture when I met Anita and her family. The whole family came for the lecture and they called me home—and it was done! I got married in 1982. She was eighteen and I was twenty-three,' he remembers fondly. Anita is an acclaimed ghazal and Sufi singer. She too has a law degree, but has preferred a career in music. She had her first solo show at the celebrated Shridharani Art Gallery in 1993 in Delhi.

Soon after their marriage, Abhishek left for Cambridge for a second time, and this time Anita accompanied him. 'It is true that some people are born with a silver spoon. But they need to fight hard to prove themselves in whatever career they choose. Being the son of a famous lawyer clearly gives you a push. But comparisons are always drawn. If you do not work hard enough and if you are not able to prove yourself, the system rejects you,' he says plainly.

The actual test of a person's potential comes when they start to perform. 'Choosing the right branch of law proved to be more confusing than I had expected. Prior to entering the profession, I had a weird and mysterious fascination with excise law. So I joined the best-known expert in that subject: Ravinder Narain. My romanticism for excise law probably had roots in my ignorance of the subject, and hence I left within a few months,' he says.

'"Much can be achieved if the decibels are kept low." That's the way my father reacted to counter a judge's ire in one of his arguments in the Supreme Court. "I am not used to shouting and countering with vociferous arguments. I am always for a polite conversation between the bench and the Bar," my father used to say. I think I have inherited that trait from him, though I may sometimes come across as more aggressive. Normally, I am relatively calm while arguing my cases. Amidst all the excitement, I am able to exercise a lot of restraint in the courtroom, and my restraint is principled. I find the exchange of hot words between the judges and lawyers quite painful,' he says. But he adds, 'I don't let sarcasm or insults by opposing parties go unrebutted.'

Abhishek's father passed away on 6 October 2007, leaving a deep void in his son's life.

As a Jurist

Abhishek, in his legal career, has served as the Additional Solicitor General (ASG) of India and as vice president of the Supreme Court Bar Association. He has also been one of the foremost senior lawyers of the country, designated as a senior advocate by the Supreme Court. He has been at the forefront of several landmark decisions of the Supreme Court on constitutional law, commercial law and several other areas of civil law, including (as amicus curiae) in the *D.K. Basu* decision on custodial deaths in 1997, Naveen Jindal's right-to-fly-the-tricolour case, the commercial free speech case involving the Tata Press Yellow Pages in 1995, the *NTC Bombay Mills* case on urban environmental issues, the *Mandal* case on reservation for backward classes, matters of mental-asylum reform (as amicus curiae), the *Renusagar* cases on international commercial arbitration, Badal's case dealing with the Prevention of Corruption Act, 1988, and the Delhi and Mumbai airports privatization case, amongst several others. But the one case that holds lasting charm for him in terms of its mass appeal is the *National Flag* case.

Abhishek represented industrialist-politician Naveen Jindal and got him, along with over a billion other Indians, the right to fly the national flag atop their houses—something that had been earlier restricted to government buildings only.

Lawyers Jayant Nath, Ciccu Mukhopadhaya and Najmi Waziri worked with him for many years in their formative years of legal practice. Nath and Waziri are now Delhi High Court judges, and Mukhopadhaya a designated senior.

In the 1990s, Abhishek had a flourishing practice, and it would double with every passing year. Another important thing that happened then was that he was appointed an amicus curiae to assist the judges. 'It all happened when I was arguing in the Supreme Court—the case of a poor, unemployed serviceman, Teja Singh, from Chandigarh. His services had been terminated and his house was being taken over. The matter came up before a very tough judge, Justice Chinnappa Reddy. He ultimately dismissed the case and did not give us much relief, but he was impressed by the arguments made by me and instantly developed a liking for me. And out of the blue, one day, he appointed me as amicus,' relates Abhishek.

In the case of *Renusagar Power Plant Co. Ltd v. General Electric Co* (AIR 1994 SC 860) (the *Renusagar* case), the Supreme Court, while construing the term 'public policy' in Section 7(1)(b)(ii) of the Foreign Awards (Recognition and Enforcement) Act, 1961, applied the principles of arbitration and private international law and held that an award would be deemed contrary to public policy if such enforcement was contrary to the fundamental policy of Indian law or the interests of India or justice or morality, and that it cannot be set aside on merits.

Later, Abhishek argued *National Thermal Power Corp. v. Singer Company*, both before the single judge and the Division Bench in the Delhi High Court, but senior counsel Shanti Bhushan led him in the Supreme Court and allowed him to do part of the rejoinder while he sat next to Abhishek. Justice T.K. Thommen, who was heading the bench, also wanted to hear him as a junior counsel.

Becoming a Senior

At the age of thirty-four, Abhishek was designated as India's youngest senior advocate ever. He has handled all sorts of matters from criminal to arbitration and service matters to the fight between the two Ambani brothers over natural gas. The range is too large. But telecom has been a special field for him. For the past twenty years, he has been involved in all the major telecom cases, right from their inception, including the 2G spectrum case as well as the CAG audit into the accounts of all telecom companies. Four big issues—CDMA- and GSM-technology-related arguments, revenue share and one-time spectrum-charge-related cases, the Vodafone tax imbroglio and the 2G scam—have shaped the course of the telecom industry. Besides, he has also been handling all major IPR matters, straddling the entire gamut of trademarks, patents, copyright and designs.

'My representation has been almost always on the side of various leading private telecom companies including Bharti, Vodafone and Idea Cellular on three major issues: charge of one-time spectrum fees, the 3G intra-circle roaming agreement and licence renewals. The combined financial impact of these telecom cases may accrue to around Rs 1,20,000 crore. It was during my tenure as Congress spokesperson that I had to fight against the government in several telecom cases. I genuinely believe and assert that the legal profession, for any top practitioner, must remain different from one's political career. Nevertheless, I must say that I have a list of over seventy high-profile corporate cases aggregating to over Rs 50 crore as fees, approximately, which I have refused purely because of perceived conflict with my role as a senior Congress leader, though I still believe that I am and was fully entitled to appear in them,' he says.

'There is no reason to point a finger at Singhvi if he represents against the government. He is an officer of the court and he has to argue for whoever appoints him,' was BJP leader Piyush Goyal's defence recently. He is now the power minister. Over the years, Abhishek's arguments have influenced the way the telecom industry has evolved. It was in 1993–94 that his long and influential journey in telecom litigation began.

'My father has been my role model. He was multifaceted, highly versatile, and a great orator in both English and Hindi. The young and very dynamic and articulate late Congress leader Madhavrao Scindiaji, who died in September 2001 in a plane crash, has also influenced me. Another huge influence was Prakash Vir Shastri, a noted member of Parliament, for his oratory skills. President Pranab Mukherjee's consistent hard work, unfailing memory, remarkable grasp of precedents and sense of history is also inspiring,' reveals Abhishek.

Abhishek believes that a lawyer should never ever compromise on his professional ethics, and should always try to turn up for a case. He says that though he does fail sometimes, 'I kill myself trying to reach every commitment.' He believes it is important to have strong priorities to lay emphasis on important issues and to avoid doing things with ulterior motives.

As an ASG

An interesting thing happened in 1997. Madhavrao Scindia, whom Abhishek was rather close to despite their fifteen-year age gap, pushed his name for the post of ASG. Abhishek was just thirty-seven years old at the time.

The Congress wasn't at the Centre then. Scindia pressed and pushed his case, and Abhishek was finally appointed ASG. 'I was appointed in the H.D. Deve Gowda–led Janata Party government, though I was totally apolitical then. I got a call from then Union law minister, Ramakant Khalap. I said I was honoured. I was happy to receive a call from the law minister. I was only thirty-seven then and was naturally very naive about the ways of the government. I did not fully understand the way the system worked. As ASG, I handled several important cases including a petition alleging that the country suffered losses running into several thousand crores due to the arbitrary transfer of the Mukta–Panna oil fields to a joint venture of Reliance Industries and Enron from Oil and Natural Gas Corporation Limited (ONGC). The two petitioners, the Centre for Public Interest Litigation and the National Alliance of People's Movements, had alleged that the government had been paying a multinational joint venture, the Enron–Reliance consortium, thrice the market price,' he says.

Even the famous Samba spy case gave Abhishek a lot of prominence as the ASG. The issue involved a gross miscarriage of justice by the army as its various officers were implicated falsely and detained for years on the charges of spying for Pakistan.

Another petition by News TV India Ltd, the representative of STAR TV in India, that hogged the limelight during Abhishek's tenure as ASG, was a challenge to a government notification that banned the use of direct-to-home (DTH) telecast equipment. He faced Kapil Sibal, now a senior lawyer and former telecom minister, on the opposite side, arguing that the ban imposed on the use of DTH equipment for receiving frequencies of 4800MHz and above violated the fundamental right to information enshrined in the Indian Constitution.

It was also just before this time that Abhishek also handled the high-profile JMM MPs' bribery case. The CBI had registered FIRs against JMM MPs Suraj Mandal, Shibu Soren, Simon Marandi and Shailendra Mahato for their alleged bribing of Opposition parliamentarians to have them vote against a no-confidence motion on 28 July 1993, against the Narasimha Rao government. 'In August 1997, I returned the case on my own,' reveals Abhishek. 'Professional ethics—that's what the practice should embody. However, it's quite unfortunate that our Bar seems to lack this. The Bar is often a classic case of preaching without practice,' he says.

Abhishek was elected the vice president of the Supreme Court Bar Association in 1999. He fought for its presidentship in 2009, but lost his campaign. 'Today, there is a complete dichotomy; dichotomy between your excellence, stature and standing at the Bar versus your ability to get elected. Take the top ten advocates of this country. Then take the top twenty. Then take the top thirty. And multiply that over twenty-five years. In twenty years, the top ten, twenty, thirty lawyers would not even seek elections to the Bar, or would not be electable. Conversely, the people who are elected and are electable are not part of the elite list because they have nothing to do with the practice;

they have often not even entered the courtroom, so this can't be right. I think it is important that the terms are limited,' he says.

As Congress Spokesperson

Congress Party president, Sonia Gandhi, appointed Abhishek as the official spokesperson, a role which he has now been handling for more than fifteen years. Ms Gandhi had her reasons, and Abhishek had the merit. It is interesting that Dr L.M. Singhvi was in the BJP, while his son, Abhishek Manu Singhvi, joined the Congress.

The father–son duo, despite their different political leanings, had excellent personal relations. They found enough Chinese whisperers and tattlers in each party trying to malign them and sow seeds of suspicion about them in both places. 'These kinds of things happen in politics. Detractors endowed with idleness practise only this brand of politics. Before becoming the Congress spokesperson, I was offered bigger roles by two parties, the BJP and the NCP [Nationalist Congress Party], both as spokesperson,' he says.

A Typical Day

Abhishek sleeps only about five to five-and-a-half hours a night, and does a lot of things at home. He clears his emails, reads all his files and tries to go for a walk for an hour in the morning. But it does not happen as regularly as he would like.

His typical day is fascinating, and he skilfully handles all his tasks with dazzling efficiency—managing several heavy court matters, press conferences, Parliament speeches, TV interviews, all on the same day. 'Multitasking has always been the bane and joy of my life,' he remarks.

Abhishek has been honoured by being asked to be the opening batsman for almost every important parliamentary debate after his election to the Rajya Sabha in 2006—including discussions relating to office of profit, the Indo-US nuclear agreement, replying to the President's motion of thanks, the Union Budget, the Lokpal, the Ayodhya/Babri Masjid/Liberhan report, internal security, the National Judicial Appointments Commission, several law-related bills, and so on. He was appointed chairman of the Parliamentary Standing Committee on Law and Justice in his first term itself—a rarity.

Abhishek generally returns to his home office by 5.30 p.m., after which he attends legal conferences and appears on TV news debates as the Congress spokesperson. Despite the challenging schedule, he tries to eat dinner by 9 p.m. 'I am very conscious of the tasks I am performing, and a high degree of alertness helps me perform to my utmost satisfaction. I also make basic notes for every case, and that helps me recall key details at a later stage. This note-making is extremely important, so that I don't have to reinvent the wheel. A notebook, I feel, is more important than a laptop,' he says.

Setback

In April 2012, Abhishek resigned from his prestigious profile of being the Congress spokesperson for a while and also resigned as the chairperson of the Parliamentary Standing Committee on Law and Justice due to allegations of personal indiscretion. Abhishek believes he was attacked only for his strong media profile. He says he saw the pits of human nature during those trying days. Everyone with ulterior motives and axes to grind joined the act. Several complaints to Bar associations were filed from behind the scenes by these persons, and even PILs were filed! All were rejected.

'I am unlikely to ever forgive or forget. I am no Gandhiji,' says Abhishek candidly. 'I could not consider my education complete without a degree from the University of Adversity.'

The sinister sides of technology and sensationalism are what he considered to be the architects of the infamous sex scandal. He felt himself being dragged into a political controversy, so before it got murkier, he simply resigned, saying he was not attracted to posts.

'The facets of human nature I saw were absolutely disgusting. I felt very caustic; I felt that everything I was looking at was hypocritical, farcical and a pretence. My faith in the essential goodness of human nature vanished. Fortunately, some of it has been restored,' he says, adopting a dismissive view of the episode, and viewing it as an act to create an imbalance in his personal, professional and political life.

There was another controversy where Abhishek was reprimanded by the Congress high command, and was asked, for a short while, to not brief the media. This was regarding the Kerala State Lottery controversy, where Abhishek was arguing for a lottery baron.

'Arguing for the lottery baron was unethical,' a state Congress leader proclaimed, obviously with no knowledge of the legal system or the ethical principles binding senior advocates. Ironically, the Kerala lottery case involved Abhishek defending a central act passed by the UPA! 'Nobody has to teach me about Congress's values,' was Abhishek's retaliation to critics.

Apart from these raging controversies, Abhishek has been very upright and upfront in his approach and attitude.

Hall of Legal Fame

Dr Abhishek Manu Singhvi is an Indian politician belonging to the Indian National Congress, and a member of Parliament, representing Rajasthan in the Rajya Sabha. He is an eminent jurist, parliamentarian, media personality, columnist, author and commentator.

It was unquestionably his legal brilliance that helped him become the youngest ASG in India at the age of thirty-seven. Professionally, he believes that a lawyer should neither choose clients nor judge them. 'It's difficult to do so and still fulfil my sense of justice,' he says. He reveals that he initially says no if he has to, but if and when he takes up a case, he stays with it all the way, and does his work with vigour and with no regrets.

'When I make a point before the bench, my job is to ensure that the judge fully understands the issue, that my clients are represented in the best light, that I do so without suppression or misstatement of facts. Then I leave the case with the judge and forget about the outcome,' says Abhishek, summing up his general approach. He lives by the mantra of not carrying the baggage of cases in one's mind.

Speed, comprehension of issues and delivery of arguments in a coherent, logical and pithy manner of presentation are extremely important for him. He believes that future lawyers will be more specialized, much more tech-savvy, and will make better lawyers, but lesser advocates.

Mood, direction, philosophy, momentum and the pace of a judge—all are vital for success. Abhishek feels that all these elements may be considered as elements of court craft. To be crafty, however, is something to be avoided, as it doesn't serve one well in the long run.

Lawyer Keshav Mohan, who often briefs Abhishek for matters, says, 'I feel that he is one of the most intelligent lawyers I have ever briefed. He understands and picks up important details in any complex case quickly and argues it on the first principle, starting with the interpretation of the law. He can go to any extent for his client and will not give up till the last moment.'

Abhishek lays great emphasis on 'preparedness'—both 'case preparedness' and 'court preparedness' are vital to him. Case preparedness relates to being a good lawyer and a good advocate. To be both is the ideal, but a challenge. Good advocates need not be good lawyers and vice versa.

For Abhishek, content comes first, followed by sequencing— putting across one's point combatively, but without fighting with the judge. 'When you argue before a judge, what helps is the sequence, the logic behind each point, your readiness for the next query and a general feel of where and in which direction the judge is going,' he says. He puts great emphasis on the rejoinder. 'More cases are won or lost on rejoinders than most lawyers realize.'

Abhishek's association with the media has been noted for a long time. His communication skills are acknowledged to be outstanding and have also led to him delivering lectures at the most eminent international universities like Harvard, Stanford, Yale, George Washington University, and so on. He is an active communicator with a good sense of humour, which influences his listeners to a great extent.

Having been honoured with the Global Leader of Tomorrow Award in 1999 at the World Economic Forum (Davos) at the age of forty-two, Abhishek has been an inspiring role-model for youngsters. His contribution to the field of media includes 'Candid Corner', a column written by him for several years in the *Hindustan Times*. His columns have also been compiled into a book and published in 2006 as *Candid Corner: Reflections of Abhishek Singhvi*, with a foreword written by former prime minister Dr Manmohan Singh.

In 2007, Abhishek was invited to deliver a lecture on the issue of federalism; his speech was printed in the prominent *IIPA Journal*, apart from being declared the best essay. Abhishek also taught at St John's College, Cambridge, while getting a PhD, and also completed the Program of Instruction for Lawyers (a short summer programme) from Harvard, USA. He has lectured to student/faculty groups and general audiences at universities, to NGOs as well as think tanks (like the Heritage Foundation, the International Council of World Affairs, etc.) and also participated in several international conferences in locations ranging from Paris to Pakistan.

Abhishek has been conferred honorary Doctor of Law degrees from Amity University, Rajasthan, and Jain Vishwa Bharati University.

His interests include reading autobiographies and biographies; his favourites include *A Sparrow's Flight* by Lord Quintin Hogg Hailsham, *Long Walk to Freedom* by Nelson Mandela, *Napoleon* by Vincent Cronin, and so on. He is always on the lookout for biographies of great men with outstanding talent, and real-life stories of people overcoming remarkable obstacles and fighting back. His other interests are Hindi-film music, watching action thrillers and travelling. His dream is to initiate processes and programmes that would ensure real and genuine comprehensive changes in India.

THE CASE

Reliance Industries Limited v. Union of India
Judgement by bench comprising Justices Surinder Singh Nijjar and A.K Sikri delivered on 23 May 2014.

The Mukesh Ambani–led Reliance Industries Ltd (RIL) finally received big relief. The Supreme Court accepted its stand that English courts only had the jurisdiction to decide its ongoing arbitration dispute with the Indian government over reimbursement of royalties and taxes in the Panna–Mukta and Tapti (PMT) gas fields, located just off the western coast of Mumbai. Besides, any final arbitral award can be challenged only in English courts, but substantive Indian arbitration laws will have to be applied by the foreign courts. While deciding the issues, the English courts must look at India's public policy, it was held.

The apex court rejected the Ministry of Petroleum and Natural Gas's stand that the matter should be settled in an Indian court as the disputes involved substantial questions affecting Indian public interest.

RIL and Enron Oil and Gas India (the predecessor to the UK-based international energy group BG Exploration and Production India Limited) and ONGC had entered into contracts with the government on 22 December 1994 for the exploration and production of petroleum from the PMT fields (discovered in 1992), the contracts being valid for twenty-five years. RIL is the largest private sector company in India, with interests in activities including the exploration and production of oil and gas, petroleum refining and marketing petrochemicals, textiles, retail and special economic zones.

Earlier in 2011, the operators had approached the government to appoint an arbitrator for reimbursement for royalties and cess paid to the government on account of differences over methods to calculate cost recovery. Since the government refused, the firms approached the Court of Arbitration, Hague.

Some awards have already been passed by the arbitrator in England. The international arbitrator in 2012 had directed the government to reimburse the companies to the tune of $11,413,172, besides additional cess recovered from them.

The arbitral tribunal comprising Christopher Lau S.C. (the chairman), Justice B.P. Jeevan Reddy, former judge of the Supreme Court of India and Peter Leaver, QC, is hearing the matter. Aggrieved by the foreign award, the government moved the Delhi High Court, which in March 2013 favoured the government's stand that in the event the arbitration award was sought to be enforced outside India, it would render Indian entities remediless.

Quashing the Delhi High Court's order, the Supreme Court said that the High Court had committed a 'jurisdictional error' as the parties to the production-sharing contract (PSC) had 'consciously agreed' for arbitration in London to resolve any dispute.

The High Court also held that undoubtedly the governing law of the contract, i.e. proper law of the contract, is the law of India, and that the same would be applicable. Therefore, the parties never intended to altogether exclude the laws of India, so far as contractual rights are concerned. The laws of England would be applicable only with regard to the curial law matters, i.e., conduct of the arbitral proceedings, and not for other purposes.

It further held that the fiscal laws of India cannot be derogated from and, therefore, the exclusion of Indian public policy was not envisaged by the parties at the time of entering into the contract.

The High Court then concluded that the public policy of India cannot be adjudged under the laws of England.

According to the High Court, the disputes involved rights in rem. Therefore, due regard has to be given to Indian laws. An award which is said to be against public policy can be permitted to be challenged in India even though the seat of arbitration is outside India. The High Court also took support from the doctrine of public trust with regard to natural resources, saying that since the companies were seeking refund of the amount of cess, royalties and service tax—all matters of public money in India—the jurisdiction of the Indian courts cannot be excluded.

Impact

The arbitration scene in India is changing, with the courts becoming increasingly hesitant to exercise control over foreign arbitrations. This judgement is another step in this direction. The judges have taken a clear stand to oust the jurisdiction of Indian courts over an ongoing foreign arbitration proceeding by keeping in mind the inconveniences that were likely to be caused.

The Supreme Court said that the conclusion reached by the High Court would lead to the chaotic situation where the parties would be left rushing between India and England for redressal of their grievances.

This judgement is also significant because it explicitly recognizes the need to follow international trends embodied in the UNCITRAL Model Law and the New York Convention.

The laws of India have been made applicable to the substantive contract. The laws of England govern the dispute resolution mechanism. The provision for arbitration is a deliberate election of remedy other than the usual remedy of a civil suit. The alternative dispute resolution (ADR) mechanism under the arbitral laws of different nations is legally and jurisprudentially accepted, sanctified by the highest law-making bodies of the member states, signatories to the New York Convention. India is not only a signatory to the New York Convention, but it has also taken into account the UNCITRAL Model Laws and the UNCITRAL rules, whilst enacting the Arbitration and Conciliation Act, 1996 (the Arbitration Act). Therefore, it would not be possible to accept the submission of the government that the law of the contract is also the law of the arbitration agreement.

After analysing the PSC to discover the real intention of the parties as to whether the provisions of the Arbitration Act have been excluded, the top court said that the proper law of the contract is Indian law, and that the proper law of the arbitration agreement is the law of England.

The judges said that it was too late in the day to contend that the seat of arbitration is not analogous to an exclusive jurisdiction clause. Once the parties had consciously agreed that the juridical seat of the arbitration would be London and that the arbitration agreement will be governed by the laws of England, it was no longer open to them to contend that the provisions of Part I of the Arbitration Act would also be applicable to the arbitration agreement.

The mere fact that the question of Indian public interest was involved was not sufficient to attract the applicability of the statute.

The government, through senior counsel A.K. Ganguly, contended that in order to determine whether the Arbitration Act was excluded, the contract had to be seen as a whole. Here, the contract is in India, for the work to be done in India over twenty-five years; secondly, it deals with natural resources; the Union of India is a trustee of these resources for the citizens of India. London was designated as the seat of arbitration only to provide a certain comfort to the foreign parties. The contract cannot be read in such a way so as to exclude the Arbitration Act, it said.

Winning Strokes

Dr Abhishek Manu Singhvi, appearing for the contractors, submitted that the issue of 'arbitrability' is governed by the law of the seat of arbitration. The seat of the arbitration being England, the issue of arbitrability is governed by English law. He raised a preliminary objection to the maintainability of the government's petition, primarily on the ground that by choosing English law to govern their agreement to arbitration and expressly agreeing to London-seated arbitration, the parties have excluded the application of Part I of the Arbitration Act. Thus, the Delhi High Court had no jurisdiction to entertain the objection filed by the government under Section 34 of the Arbitration Act. It was emphasized by him that the courts of England and Wales have exclusive jurisdiction to entertain any challenge to the award.

According to Abhishek, the provisions of Part I of the Arbitration Act are necessarily excluded, being wholly inconsistent with the arbitration agreement which provides 'that the arbitration agreement shall be governed by English law'. Thus, the remedy of the government to challenge any award rendered in the arbitration proceedings would lie under the relevant provisions contained in the Arbitration Act, 1996, of England and Wales, according to him.

Abhishek opposed Ganguly's arguments that the issues involved here relate to the violation of the public policy of

India, holding that such submissions run against the well-settled law in India as well as other jurisdictions.

Abhishek stated that all the disputes raised by his clients were contractual in nature and that the performance of any of these obligations would not lead to any infringement of any of the laws of India per se, as argued by the government.

IV

ARVIND P. DATAR: NEVER GIVE UP

Born on 26 September 1956 in Mumbai

Whatever you vividly imagine, ardently desire, sincerely believe and enthusiastically act upon must inevitably come to pass.
—Paul J. Meyer

THE LAST sentence of the application form was particularly traumatic. It dashed all his hopes of joining the merchant navy, becoming a captain and then owning a shipping company someday—a big shipping company. He had even gone to the extent of naming his prospective company Disco—or Datar International Shipping Company. 'It was there before me . . . and in a moment it was all gone. The last sentence . . . and my desire to fulfil my cherished dream was over,' says Arvind Datar, one of India's leading corporate and tax lawyers today, recounting what undoubtedly was one of the worst days of his life. A major surgery in his final year at school had medically disqualified him. It was a big setback, but looking back, he has no regrets, for he thoroughly enjoys arguing cases before the Supreme Court and the High Courts.

The Background

Arvind's father was in the merchant navy. He had worked as a captain for the Scindia Steam Navigation Company. In 1961, he set up his own business in Chennai. It was this decision that made the family relocate to that city. Arvind was born in Mumbai in

1956 and did his initial schooling in a Marathi-medium school. He would have continued his studies in Chennai till class seven, had the anti-Hindi agitation in 1967 not taken an ugly turn. As a result, Arvind's parents were worried and debated the possibility of going back to Mumbai.

In this uncertainty, one unanimous decision emerged. The parents decided to send their son to a boarding school. In 1968, Arvind joined a boarding school in Pune, the Shri Shivaji Preparatory Military School. His school days shaped his personality to a great extent. It nurtured his desire to excel. He finished his schooling in 1972, standing first in his school, first in Maharashtra in social studies and also winning the school's Mohan Dharia scholarship. Arvind has happy memories of his four-year stint in Pune, although he has lost touch with almost all his schoolmates. However, it's his law college friends that he has been able to keep meeting frequently.

The Tryst with a Twist

Unable to join the merchant navy, Arvind's passion ensured he worked hard to prepare for marine engineering and so he joined the pre-university course at Vaishnav College, Chennai, and studied for the IIT entrance exams. Soon, a second medical calamity struck. Unfortunately, that year, Arvind had a serious intestinal twist, which became critical, but he miraculously escaped a major surgery. 'He shouldn't be staying away from home,' was the doctor's advice.

However, despite his health condition, Arvind had made up his mind to join Ramnarain Ruia College in Mumbai for a BSc (Hons) degree in physics and mathematics. The two medical setbacks had unsettled Arvind to a great extent and he was quite unsure of what to do next.

Becoming a Lawyer

Arvind continued participating in debates and won several prizes, but slowly realized that he was not happy with his studies and barely managed to get his degree. But at Mumbai, he was spellbound by the lectures of renowned lawyer Nani Palkhivala, who not only spoke on the budget but also gave lectures in various colleges. It was at this time that he decided to become not just a lawyer, but a tax lawyer.

In 1976, he graduated and moved back to Chennai to pursue the law; his parents were still settled there. The long hours of commuting in Mumbai had also played a part in his decision to move to the south. Chennai had its own share of problems. Arvind was unsure of getting admission because of reservations, not to mention that his final marks were disappointing. If not Chennai, his plan B was to return to Mumbai. Fortunately, he just about managed an admission into the Madras Law College.

Having decided to become a tax lawyer, Arvind now wanted an additional degree in accountancy. But the question on his mind was whether he should pursue chartered accountancy or cost accountancy.

'Chartered accountancy would mean travelling and touring for audits, and this would have impacted my law studies. Instead, I opted for cost-accounting conducted by the Institute of Cost & Works Accountants of India,' he recalls. Only six students, including Arvind, had cleared all three groups of the intermediate course, and Madras Fertilizers Ltd wanted to recruit such students as 'cost assistants'. 'The stipend paid for such a role was Rs 400 per month. It was a phenomenal amount for a graduate at that time. It was quite tempting, and I needed the money. But I was firm on becoming a lawyer,' Arvind recounts.

He had joined the Madras Law College in 1976. This was during the Emergency in 1975–77, and there were no strikes in the first year. Classes were conducted on a regular basis, and the first year of law college was perhaps the best year of his college life. The college had excellent lecturers, most of whom were practising lawyers who taught only part-time. The classes on contract law, transfer of property and evidence were truly outstanding.

After 1977, when the Emergency was lifted, complete chaos ensued and the college was plagued by frequent strikes. In his final year, Arvind's classes were on for only fifty-four days. 'The last two years of law college were the worst in my life and a terrible waste of time. However, this gave me time for my cost-accountancy course and also to write a small book,' he says.

Two important things happened during this period in Arvind's life. One, he started his own publishing concern, Delta Publishing Company. And second, he wrote his first book, *Preparation for MBA Entrance Exams*. Two of his friends were at IIM Ahmedabad and XLRI, Jamshedpur, and they helped him write it. 'It was basically a collection of objective English and mathematics tests. The book was reprinted in two editions and yielded reasonable profits, but is out of print now,' he says with pride.

The frequent strikes in college also gave him additional time to write the book and even go from bookshop to bookshop selling the book in Chennai, Mumbai and Pune. Advertised in the then popular *Illustrated Weekly of India*, the sales for the book in other parts of the country were carried out through VPP (India Post's value payable post).

At law college, Arvind also involved himself extensively in debates, where his team won a record number of prizes. He also participated in moot court competitions.

In 1977, Arvind and a fellow classmate Aryama Sundaram (featured later in this book), went to Pondicherry to take part in an international law moot-court competition, but they did not win any prize.

In 1979, Arvind, along with another classmate, A. Gunaseelan, went all the way to Chandigarh for a moot court competition and won the third prize. When they returned to Chennai, the acting principal refused to reimburse their expenses. Therefore, two days after he enrolled as an advocate in February 1980, Arvind filed a suit against the Madras Law College in the Small Causes Court at Chennai for the recovery of Rs 654, which was the expenditure for going to Chandigarh to attend the moot-court competition. 'I waited till my enrolment because I did not want to risk the law college withholding my "good conduct" certificate. I was the plaintiff and also went into the witness box,' Arvind recalls. The suit was decreed, and he later went with the bailiff to attach the furniture of the law college. At that point, the law college reimbursed Rs 654 to him, with interest, which came to about Rs 700!

The Madras Law College is housed in a beautiful building, and Arvind feels sad when he sees how strikes and other factors have slowly destroyed this great institution. The college boasts of eminent alumni including several pre- and post-Independence High Court judges that include Sir Alladi Krishnaswamy Iyer, Sir C.P. Ramaswamy Aiyar and, later, well-known lawyers such as M.K. Nambiar (who argued the *A.K. Gopalan* case), K. Parasaran, K.K. Venugopal, former Attorney General G. Ramaswamy and former ASG V.P. Raman. Almost all the Supreme Court judges from Tamil Nadu are products of the Madras Law College.

Arvind used to attend college till 1 p.m., and from 1.30–4 p.m. he would go to his friend's press to check and revise proofs. After the book was printed, the afternoons were spent dispatching the book to vendors and other sales-related chores. As the sole-proprietor-cum-sole-employee, this took considerable time, and Arvind's younger brother also lent a helping hand. Thereafter, he would swim for an hour and then attend his cost-accountancy

classes. That was his regular schedule for two years. After joining
the legal profession, Arvind transferred the proprietorship concern
to his mother, and for the past thirty-five years, his mother has
printed and published a useful calendar-cum-almanac.

In 1982, Arvind completed his cost accountancy course. At
the time, his father's ex-employer, the Scindia Steam Navigation
Company, advertised for the post of accounts officer, for which
fresh chartered accountants and cost accountants alone were
eligible. The salary was a princely sum of Rs 2250 per month. In
contrast, Arvind was earning Rs 300 per month as a junior at the
Bar. 'The offer was irresistible. And my father asked me if I wanted
to join the shipping company. Obviously, he was worried at the
relatively minor sum his twenty-six-year-old son was earning,'
he recalls. Arvind told him that there was no question of him
quitting the legal profession, saying, 'Even if I have to beg, I will
do it in the High Court.' He had already planned to practise civil
law for one year and then specialize in taxation for three years.
On exactly the fourth year after his enrolment, Arvind planned to
set up his independent practice. There was simply no question of
taking up any job.

Accordingly, after his enrolment in February 1980, Arvind
joined the office of Mrs Ramani Natarajan, who had a civil and
writ practice. After fifteen months, he joined the office of M/s
Subbaraya Aiyar, Padmanabhan and Ramamani, which was then
the leading tax law firm in South India. His senior was K.R.
Ramamani.

On 1 March 1984, as planned, Arvind set up his independent
practice with just Rs 300 in his savings account. He married
Himani in November 1983—a bold decision, considering the
little money he had then. Fortunately, he lived with his parents
and, therefore, expenses for the young couple were comparatively
less. However, he did not want to change his plan and decided

to take the plunge regardless of the difficulties. Contrary to his hopes, this was the beginning of a long period of very little work and almost five years of serious struggle.

Blessed with Excellent Mentors

'I was blessed with excellent seniors who guided me and gave me all the encouragement that was necessary in my formative years,' Arvind recollects. Mrs Ramani Natarajan allowed him to argue cases in the City Civil Court as well as the High Court, right from the beginning. Arvind remembers appearing in a civil revision petition just two days after his enrolment, and in a writ petition before Justice Mohan (who later came to the Supreme Court) in August 1980, just six months after his enrolment. Similarly, Mr Ramamani, his income tax senior, was extremely supportive and allowed him to appear independently for several years before the appellate authorities including the tribunal. While Mrs Ramani Natarajan was a civil lawyer, her husband, N. Natarajan, was a leading criminal lawyer and had appeared in several landmark cases. He was also appointed as the special prosecutor in the famous Bombay Blast case, and also appeared on behalf of most of the accused in the case relating to the assassination of the late prime minister Rajiv Gandhi.

There were two important lessons that Arvind learnt from his seniors. The most important advice was given by Mr Natarajan, who said, 'It does not matter if you decide to be a cobbler; just make sure that you become the best cobbler in the world.' The other piece of advice he received was to never ever antagonize or quarrel with a judge. 'Remember, it is your client's life. For you, it is only bread and butter.' This was the advice Natarajan had received from his senior, the late S. Mohan Kumaramangalam.

While briefing other seniors in important cases, Arvind tried to understand and adopt their work habits. He was particularly

privileged to work with R. Kesava Iyengar, the father of eminent
Supreme Court advocate and former Attorney General, K.
Parasaran. It was a contempt case against *Indian Express*, and
Arvind was the junior lawyer who was to appear for the proprietor,
Ramnath Goenka, and the eminent journalist B.G. Verghese,
amongst others. As a student of the Madras Law College, which
was frequently closed due to strikes, Arvind would visit the
adjoining High Court and observe senior advocates arguing their
cases.

One lawyer he particularly admired even as a student was
R. Kesava Iyengar. Therefore, when the contempt case came up
for hearing, he decided to brief him. They worked together for
almost twenty days, and this was an unforgettable period of his
life. 'Although he was ninety-three years old at that time, his mind
was razor-sharp. He gave me invaluable advice. For example, he
told me that one should spend 60 per cent of one's time in reading
and preparation, and at least 40 per cent in thinking about the
case. Secondly, he told me that one should be completely ready
forty-eight hours before the case is taken up for the final hearing.
Thereafter, one should tie up the court files and open them up
only in court! He told me that one should stop preparing forty-
eight hours before the case, because "If you prepare endlessly,
you will be endlessly unprepared." He took on only two briefs
a month. I have not seen any other senior preparing his case as
thoroughly as he did,' Arvind recollects fondly.

Early Struggle

After he set up his independent practice, Arvind had very
little work for several months. The senior partner of his firm,
S. Padmanabhan, gave him a cheque for Rs 5000 soon after he left
in 1984, and this was what kept the newly married couple going

for a few months. While he was a junior with Ramamani, there was a suit for Rs 81 lakh filed in the Madras High Court by the Bank of India against a leading seafood exporter. As Ramamani's junior, Arvind had replied to the legal notice and also prepared the draft written statement. When he decided to set up his independent practice, Ramamani was gracious enough to tell Arvind to take this case as his independent brief. The scheduled fee came to Rs 49,200, and this was paid to him in three annual instalments! Looking back, Arvind admits he would not have survived without these generous gestures from both Padmanabhan and Ramamani.

Arvind got his break with an offer to handle cases for the Indian Express group, which had a number of money suits for the recovery of outstandings from advertising agencies. This was an important turning point. When T.N. Seetharaman, an advocate in charge of the Express group's tax disputes, who also used to brief Ramamani, found out that Arvind was setting up his independent practice, he asked him to handle the Express group's cases at the City Civil Court. This gave Arvind substantial trial experience. Another small source of income came from criminal lawyer R. Rajaram, who was Natarajan's former junior. He had a number of rent-control cases and appeals which were all heard in the Small Causes Court. As he was very busy with his criminal practice, he asked Arvind to take up these cases. Arvind was paid Rs 60–100 for a rent-control case or appeal, and did several such matters in the Small Causes Court.

During the earlier years, Arvind had very little income tax work. He did one important case for the First Leasing Company of India Ltd, and had briefed S. Govind Swaminadhan, who was the former Advocate General of Tamil Nadu as well as a fearless barrister. After this successful case, the company continued to brief Arvind for all their tax cases till it ran into financial difficulty in 2013. Indeed, as will be pointed out later, it was this company that gave Arvind the opportunity to appear in a landmark income tax case in 1998 before the Supreme Court.

Thus, after setting up his independent practice, Arvind's work was mainly before the Small Causes Court, the City Civil Court, with very few cases before the High Court.

The major reason for the limited work was Arvind's refusal to go to the office of any client or chartered accountant. He had read earlier on that legendary legal luminary K. Bhashyam Iyengar had refused to even meet the then British governor who had wanted to consult him on a personal matter. In Arvind's case, this led to a serious restriction in the number of briefs he received, as several large companies expected him to meet their managing director or chairman. Later, Arvind discussed this issue with the legendary H.M. Seervai and R. Kesava Iyengar, and both told him that what he was doing was the right thing.

Part-time Lecturer

For months, Arvind would have no work and, at times, it would become difficult to cope with the situation. These moments were short-lived setbacks. The only solace during that time came from his wife. 'There is no hurry,' she would often say.

Next in line for Arvind was teaching. When he successfully passed the Institute of Cost and Works Accountants of India (ICWAI) intermediate exam, his lecturer K.S. Anantharaman was surprised to learn that he was also studying law. He told Arvind to contact him as soon as he got done with his law course, so that he could take classes at the ICWAI.

After his enrolment, Anantharaman appointed Arvind as a part-time lecturer for commercial laws, and he taught at this institute till 1984. In 1981, he was also invited by the southern chapter of the Institute of Chartered Accountants of India and the

Institute of Company Secretaries of India to take classes on taxation and commercial/general laws, respectively. Arvind taught at these two institutes till the early 1990s. By that time, his practice had increased considerably and he no longer had the time to take classes.

Arvind also joined as a part-time lecturer at the Bharathidasan Institute of Management, Tiruchirappalli. He would travel to Tiruchirappalli from Chennai on Friday nights and take four classes each on Saturday and Sunday and then return to Chennai on Monday morning. He taught both direct and indirect taxes to the MBA students, and these lectures earned him additional money. Arvind says, 'Every junior lawyer who is serious about his practice should try and take classes on his chosen subject of specialization. I feel that I learnt more law by teaching than I did at college. For most classes, I would try to teach without notes and, therefore, would have to read extensively beforehand.' The knowledge Arvind gained while preparing for these classes has stood him in good stead till today.

Writing Articles and Books

When he joined the Bar, Arvind had set a goal for himself to write a nationally known law book by his thirtieth birthday. 'For lawyers, advertising is prohibited, and the only way a lawyer can make himself known is by writing articles and books,' he says. O.C. Mazengarb had written a small book on advocacy and had famously said: 'Get known, young man; get favourably known, if possible, but get known.' To hone his writing skills, Arvind decided to write articles, and he set himself a target of writing one article on taxation per week and, in a span of two years, wrote seventy-seven articles. Apart from bringing home additional income, the articles resulted in Arvind being invited to participate in various tax seminars.

He first attempted to write the student's edition of Seervai's commentary on the Constitution of India. K.S. Shavaksha had already written a student's edition of *Mulla's Contract Act*, and H.P. Ranina had written a students' edition of *Kanga and Palkhivala's The Law and Practice of Income Tax*. Arvind wrote to Seervai requesting permission to write the student's edition, but the legendary jurist wrote back a detailed letter explaining why a student's edition of his commentary would be impractical.

In 1984, Arvind was appearing in a winding-up case and found that A. Ramaiya's *Guide to the Companies Act* had missed out on several important cases, but found that they had been noted in the *AIR Manual*. He wrote to the Wadhwa Publishing Company at Nagpur, which had just purchased the copyright from the author. By a coincidence, K.K. Wadhwa, one of the four Wadhwa brothers, was visiting Chennai the following week and was curious to meet Arvind. 'This meeting led to a long-lasting friendship and close ties with the Wadhwa family that continues even today,' says Arvind. K.K. Wadhwa asked him to write a book on the Imports and Exports (Control) Act, 1971. After completing the manuscript, Wadhwa pointed out that the book would sell only if Arvind included practical solutions on obtaining import licences, information on how exports should be carried out and so on. 'I had no clue about the import and export procedure, and Wadhwa felt that a book containing only case law would not sell. Thus, all the work done on that book was futile. In 1985, I took up the compilation of a digest of central excise and customs cases. After completing more than 70 per cent of the work, the digest project had to be abandoned because of potential copyright litigation,' recalls Arvind. In 1986, Wadhwa asked Arvind to write a full-fledged commentary on central excise because MODVAT (Modified Value Added Tax) and the new Central Excise Tariff had been introduced that very year. Therefore, the case laws that

Arvind had read and compiled for the digest were very useful in writing *Guide to Central Excise: Law & Practice*—his first major book, which was published in 1988.

Arvind remembers that he began planning the outline and chapters of this book while on a trip from Chennai to Delhi on the Grand Trunk Express. He was due to attend the silver jubilee celebrations of the Grand Lodge of India. While his father flew to Delhi, Arvind could not afford the air ticket and travelled instead on a second-class ticket. (Arvind continues to be a keen Freemason.) 'While stuck on the upper berth of the train compartment, I planned my first book with the help of the Central Excise Act, 1944, the corresponding rules and the earlier commentary which had been written by V.J. Taraporevala,' says Arvind. His book on the subject was released on 28 November 1988. By a happy coincidence, it also happened to be his mother's birthday. Writing the book took two years of excruciating hard work. 'My wife supported me wholeheartedly and read all the proofs. For two years, I did not watch a single movie,' he reveals. The manner in which the book was written was also interesting. From 1982 onwards, Arvind would be in his office at 5.30 a.m. and would wind up for the day at 9.30 p.m. 'Even in the City Civil Court, while waiting for my case to be called, I would keep making notes from the *Excise Law Times*, a sort of journal for the book. There were no computers then and the entire manuscript had to be typed and retyped,' recalls Arvind merrily.

It is hard to believe there was no regular courier service. Posting the manuscript was not only time-consuming but also dangerous because of the possibility of the package getting lost in transit. Therefore, Arvind made it a point to hand the manuscript over to a waiter in the pantry car of the Tamil Nadu Express or the Grand Trunk Express. These trains left Chennai at night and reached Nagpur the next afternoon or evening. After delivering the manuscript in a cloth bag to the waiter, Arvind would make a call to Nagpur and inform K.K. Wadhwa of the name of the waiter. At Nagpur, Wadhwa would send his employee to the station and collect the manuscript. When the proofs were ready, they were sent back from Nagpur to Chennai through another pantry-car waiter. On all these trips to the stations, Arvind would be accompanied by his wife, who would help in locating the waiter and making the STD call.

The book was the turning point in Arvind's legal career. In the first year of its publication, Arvind's professional income quadrupled and he soon had a large practice in excise and customs cases throughout South India. In due course, most of the leading companies also started regularly briefing him in excise matters.

Soon after the book was published, Wadhwa requested Arvind to edit the eleventh edition of A. Ramaiya's *Guide to the Companies Act*. Palkhivala had already expressed his inability to be the chief editor for the book and suggested the name of former Chief Justice of India J.C. Shah. Arvind gathered a team of ten lawyers from Chennai and completely updated the legal portion of the book. Justice J.C. Shah then meticulously perused these drafts and made important changes.

With the publication of this edition, Arvind's practice in company law saw a substantial increase. By a happy coincidence, the Company Law Board was created in 1991, and Arvind soon started appearing there on a regular basis. Arvind had always wanted to meet J.C. Shah, and after the publication of the new edition of Ramaiya's book, Arvind went to Mumbai to meet J.C. Shah. En route to the city, he was informed that the great judge had passed away the previous day. To his eternal regret, Arvind was ultimately not able to meet the man who had so meticulously edited and revised the work done by Arvind and his colleagues.

In 1996, Arvind began writing his commentary on the Constitution of India. His publisher was keen that the work be restricted to one volume and asked him to concentrate only on Supreme Court cases. 'But my book suffered a major setback when my computer was hit by the Chernobyl virus and the entire draft was wiped out. Unfortunately, some chapters could not be saved and had to be rewritten, thereby delaying the book by several months. It was eventually published in 2001, and the second edition was published in 2007 in three volumes,' Arvind says. The third edition is expected later this year.

The great jurist Nani Palkhivala passed away in 2002. His biography was written by M.V. Kamath, and the Palkhivala Trust requested former Attorney General Soli Sorabjee and Arvind to write a book that would chronicle Palkhivala's legal journey. They had to cover all the important cases that he had argued. 'This was a completely different project and I had to interview several retired judges and senior lawyers and chartered accountants who had worked closely with Palkhivala. This book brought me in close touch with Palkhivala's younger brother, Behram, and his family,' Arvind says. Due to a heavy workload and involvement in other books, the book titled *Nani Palkhivala: The Courtroom Genius* was eventually published in 2012. It was released in Mumbai by the then Chief Justice of India, Justice S.H. Kapadia. The book continues to sell very well and is hugely popular among law students.

The ninth edition of Kanga and Palkhivala's commentary on the *The Law and Practice of Income Tax* was published in 2003. The publishers asked Arvind to work on the tenth edition. 'This was a Herculean task as it required covering eighty-seven volumes of the income tax reports. Further, the possibility of the Income Tax Act, 1961, being replaced by the new Direct Taxes Code created uncertainty about the future of the project. Ultimately, the publishers decided to go ahead with the tenth edition and it was released in January 2014,' he says. Arvind credits the success of this edition to the excellent support he got from the large team of advocates and chartered accountants who worked on the initial drafts of the book.

Becoming a Senior

Arvind was designated as a senior advocate of the Madras High Court in July/August 2000—just one month short of his forty-fourth birthday. It is common practice and tradition for lawyers to formally apply to become a senior. Although Arvind had a very large practice by this time, he refused to apply to become a senior. One day, G. Masilamani, the then ASG of India for the southern region, asked Arvind why he had not become a senior yet. When Arvind informed him that he did not wish to apply, Masilamani told him that he proposed to suggest his name for designation as a senior advocate. At the full-court meeting of the Madras High Court, Arvind's name was unanimously approved. Thus began a new chapter in Arvind's life at the Bar.

As a senior, Arvind had to shut down his office as he was now not allowed to file any case or draft pleadings. 'I informed my juniors that they were now free to set up their own practice and I also informed my clients that they would have to make alternative arrangements as I would not be able to represent them any more. I am very happy that all the juniors have managed to do well in their careers, and most have established a large practice in Chennai,' he says.

Arvind finds that the younger generation is far brighter than him. He opines that many of them have the potential to become leaders at the Bar in the years ahead.

Important Cases

Arvind's first major case was in 1998, before Justice Sujata V. Manohar at the Supreme Court, on the issue of leasing. It was a very important income tax case, and it resulted in major tax benefits for several leasing companies as they were held eligible for investment allowance even though the leasing companies did not manufacture any goods themselves. This issue first came before the Madras Bench of the Income Tax Appellate Tribunal, where Nani Palkhivala had appeared for the assessee. Arvind vividly remembers going to the tribunal at 9.30 a.m. so as to reserve a place for himself in the court hall. He still remembers the soft-spoken arguments of Palkhivala and the manner in which he interpreted and explained the relevant statutory provisions. The department took up the matter in appeal before the Madras High Court, and in 1993, Arvind asked Nani Palkhivala to appear before the Division Bench. He was unable to do so as he was in Europe to attend the funeral of J.R.D. Tata. The Division Bench refused to adjourn the case and the matter was successfully argued by Arvind before the Madras High Court. The department further appealed to the Supreme Court in 1998, where it was heard by a bench comprising Justices Sujata Manohar and D.P. Wadhwa. Arvind argued for just an hour, and the court held in favour of all the leasing companies. After this case, Arvind slowly started appearing in more cases before the apex court.

Remembering one of the more interesting cases of his career, Arvind reveals that he appeared for Michael Jackson in a suit filed against him by a prominent Chennai-based producer in the Madras High Court. The producer sought an interim injunction against the singer's concert, which was to be held in Mumbai. He wanted the singer and the organizers to furnish security for his claim for damages against Michael Jackson for breach of a contract that the singer had signed with him. After elaborate arguments, the Madras High Court refused to grant an injunction, and the historic concert took place in Mumbai. This was a major victory for Arvind as he was still not yet a senior.

Arvind has been opposed to the creation of tribunals and the stripping of the powers of the High Courts. He firmly believes that tribunals are being created only to have a parallel judiciary which can accommodate retired civil servants.

The National Company Law Tribunal (NCLT) was created in 2002. Not a single Commonwealth country has a company law tribunal as these decide disputes between private parties, which should be decided by the judiciary and not by the quasi-judicial tribunals. The Madras Bar Association once again challenged the validity of the NCLT and the National Company Law Appellate Tribunal (NCLAT) before the Madras High Court. In a landmark judgement, Justice Jaysimha Babu of the Madras High Court upheld the creation of the tribunal, but held certain provisions to be unconstitutional. The matter was taken up before the Supreme Court and referred to a Constitution Bench, which upheld the validity of the tribunals, but imposed several safeguards to ensure their independence. Despite this judgement, the Companies Act, 2013, once again created the Company Law Tribunal, deliberately ignoring the directions of the Supreme Court. The Madras Bar Association once again challenged the validity of the NCLT/NCLAT, and this was again referred to the Constitution Bench, which upheld the NCLT/NCLAT, but with certain important changes.

The National Taxation Tribunal was created under Article 323B of the Constitution. Recently, a Constitution Bench struck down several provisions of this tribunal and also laid down important criteria for the creation of tribunals.

A mention must also be made of the dispute between the Securities and Exchange Board of India (SEBI) and the Sahara group. An issue of optional fully convertible debentures (OFCDs), to the extent of Rs 24,000 crore, was made by two companies of the Sahara group. It was claimed that the debentures were not subject to the regulations of SEBI since it was not a public issue and that the Sahara companies did not intend to list the OFCDs on any stock exchange. A notice sent by SEBI was first challenged before the Allahabad High Court, but the Supreme Court directed the issue to be decided by SEBI and the Securities Appellate Tribunal. 'In an unusual turn of events, the Supreme Court directed the appeals to be heard during the summer vacation. After two weeks of hearing, the apex court delivered a landmark decision which would have an enormous impact not only on the Sahara group but on various investment schemes as well. Subsequently, this case took several twists and turns, and SEBI was forced to initiate contempt proceedings because the Sahara group did not comply with the orders of the Supreme Court. Eventually, developments led to the incarceration of Sahara chief, Subrata Roy, and two other Sahara directors who are still in jail for not having paid 5000 crore in cash, as well as a guarantee of Rs 5000 crore, which had been imposed as a condition for the grant of bail,' he says. The proceedings are still pending before the Supreme Court.

'Datar is an outstanding lawyer because of his grasp of cases, clarity of thought and legal knowledge. Besides, his interaction with, concern for and treatment of briefing lawyers show that he is a wonderful human being. He has the ability to remain unruffled in any situation, and is a constant guiding light to juniors,' says Pratap Venugopal, partner at K.J. John & Co., which briefs Arvind in the SEBI–Sahara case.

Hall of Legal Fame

Arvind Datar owes his success to his practice of setting goals, creating a plan of action and fixing deadlines. Very often, though, he misses these deadlines, and thus achieving the goals takes much longer than planned. At the same time, he believes that, 'Goal setting is extremely important and nothing of consequence can be achieved unless one sets clear targets first.' Goals are essentially dreams with deadlines and, in any field, success is never an accident. From the beginning, Arvind had planned to work for one year as a civil lawyer, spend three years in a tax office and then set up his independent practice. Similarly, he had set clear goals for writing books and articles, although due to his busy workload, he is often behind schedule. But the books would not have been written unless there was a specific goal or target to do so.

Arvind often advises his younger colleagues to take up writing and teaching as this has played a great part in whatever success he has achieved. His eternal regret is that he is not disciplined enough and is unable to say no to the several demands that people and matters make on his time.

Arvind travels extensively and has appeared in various High Courts, tribunals and statutory authorities in different states in the last thirty-five years. Despite repeated resolutions, he has been unable to cut down all the travelling he does.

Arvind is usually up by 5.30 a.m. and, while in Chennai, is soon out for a short walk with his wife; he then tries to exercise for at least four days a week. In Chennai, he is in office by 7.30 a.m., and works till 7.30 p.m. When he is in the final stages of writing any book, he puts in a couple of hours of writing before retiring for the day. Strangely, Arvind does not read newspapers in the morning, but prefers to get to them late in the evening because he believes it is best to avoid negative thoughts early in the day— which is what happens when you read the news!

A voracious reader, Arvind is particularly fond of biographies and books on management and self-help. He has been strongly influenced by Ayn Rand, Peter Drucker, Napoleon Hill, Brian

Tracy and Claude M. Bristol. In the recent past, he has also been taken in by the writings of Anthony Robbins, Joe Dispenza and David Allen. He also watches inspirational YouTube videos and TED Talks, particularly those relating to self-help, motivation and health. Among biographies and autobiographies, he particularly enjoyed reading *Roses in December* by M.C. Chagla, and the autobiographies of M.C. Setalvad and Justice Hidayatullah. The Connemara Public Library in Chennai has an excellent collection of legal biographies, and Arvind read all of them while still in college. 'I highly recommend that young law students read these biographies. The lives of great lawyers contain important lessons, and they often serve as role models for the next generation,' he says.

Arvind is fond of going to hill stations, and prefers mountains to beaches. Despite his busy schedule, Arvind and his wife make it a point to go on a holiday at least twice a year. They have travelled all over the world extensively. Arvind particularly remembers their visit to Japan. He has also built a small home in Kodaikanal and hopes to spend more time there in the years ahead. Apart from travelling, Arvind is very fond of old Hindi-film songs. Earlier, he used to watch movies, but is now unable to indulge in this pastime as much due to work pressure.

Looking back, Arvind is grateful for the wonderful time he has had at the Bar. He considers himself extremely lucky and blessed to have had excellent seniors and dedicated juniors around him. 'I have no doubt that I could not have achieved anything without the support and constant encouragement of my wife. She cheerfully bore several days of loneliness so that various books could be written. My constant travelling also kept me away from home for several days a month,' he says. Arvind's parents have also always encouraged him in his pursuits; even today, his father does the proofreading for all his books and looks after his financial affairs. In the office, Arvind has been lucky to have a dedicated staff, most of whom have been with him for over twenty-five years. He sincerely believes that one must live with an attitude of gratitude. We need only look at the hardships that several Indians face to understand how lucky we are.

Like most lawyers, Arvind is equally worried about the problem of arrears and the difficulty faced by the general public in getting justice. He feels that not enough attention is being paid to improving the working conditions in the subordinate courts of India. He feels that management principles must be applied to improve the productivity of the trial courts, where 90 per cent of the total litigation is conducted. It is virtually impossible to expect India to have a hundred judges for every million people. Despite the efforts and the directions of the Supreme Court, we still have only about twelve judges for every million people. The only way in which the backlog can be reduced is to double the productivity of the judges. This can be done by the application of principles of industrial productivity and kaizen (a Japanese business philosophy of continuous improvement of working practices, personal efficiency, and so on). The solution is not fast-track courts, mediation or the Lok Adalat. The key is to eliminate wastage of judicial time so that judges devote time only for hearing and disposal of cases. The time lost in non-productive work is enormous. Recently, Arvind analysed the working of the City Civil Court in Chennai and found that hardly three hours per day are spent on actual trials, and a lot of precious time is wasted in calling cases and giving adjournments.

As a parting thought, Arvind sums up his life: 'At the end of the day, we have been very blessed. I couldn't ask for more. I generally have had a wonderful life.'

THE CASE

Sahara India Real Estate Corporation Ltd and Sahara Housing Investment Corporation Ltd v. Securities and Exchange Board of India

Judgement delivered by Justices K.S. Radhakrishnan and J.S. Khehar on 31 August 2012

Case Details

This is the most important judgement of recent times, and has been closely watched all over the world.

In a landmark judgement that sent clear signals to corporates to not mess with rules and regulations, the Supreme Court directed the Subrata Roy–led Sahara group companies to refund about Rs 24,000 crore (with 15 per cent interest), collected from 3.3 crore investors within three months. The companies—Sahara India Real Estate Corporation Ltd (SIRECL) and Sahara Housing Investment Corporation Ltd (SHICL)—had collected the amount through OFCDs (housing bonds) between 13 March 2008 and 16 October 2009, in violation of the law of the land.

The companies had decided to issue unsecured OFCDs by way of private placements, and filed details in the Red Herring Prospectus with the Registrar of Companies, Kanpur. SIRECL specifically indicated that it did not intend to get their securities listed on any stock exchange. Taking advantage of the loopholes in investment laws, the group stated that the scheme was open to those persons who were associated or affiliated in any manner with the Sahara group. The funds raised by the company would be utilized for financing the acquisition of townships, residential apartments, shopping complexes, etc. Construction activities would be undertaken by the company in the major cities of the country and would also finance other commercial activities or projects taken up by the company within or apart from the above projects. The company decided to carry out infrastructural projects in the country with the money.

According to the documents produced before the court, SIRECL and SHICL had garnered Rs 19,400 crore and Rs 6380 crore, respectively, within a short span of four years from the public through its vast network. The alleged fraud came to light when one Roshan Lal, a public-spirited person belonging to Uttar Pradesh, lodged a complaint with market regulator, SEBI, alleging that the group was issuing housing bonds without complying with rules issued by the Reserve Bank of India and National Housing Bank.

Upon questioning, Enam Securities Private Ltd, the merchant banker that managed the funds, replied on 29 January 2010 that SIRECL and SHICL were not registered with any stock exchange and were not subject to any rules, regulations, guidelines, notifications and directions framed by the regulator. It stated that the bonds were sold adhering to rules under the Companies Act.

After a marathon hearing, the apex court held that the collection of such huge funds by selling the bonds was illegal, and both the companies were asked to return the money.

Roy, who claimed that the Sahara group had Rs 1,50,000 crore in assets, neither obeyed the judgement pronounced on 31 August 2012, nor did he respond to several notices served by SEBI, which then moved the top court and initiated contempt of court proceedings.

On 3 March 2014, sixty-five-year-old Roy was remanded to judicial custody and sent to Tihar Jail. He was asked to deposit Rs 10,000 crore with SEBI as a bail condition. The court took a serious view of the attitude of Roy as lakhs of people who had deposited the money were suffering.

On 6 May 2014, the Supreme Court in its 207-page judgement turned down the bail plea of Subrata Roy and its two directors, who have been in jail since 4 March 2014 for failing to refund investors' money. The same evening, Justice Khehar sent a note to the Supreme Court Registry, directing it not to include him in any new bench. Justice Khehar also directed the registry that in the future, no matter pertaining to any Sahara group company should be placed before a bench of which he is a part.

Even the 6 May judgement talks of pressure, pointing to litigants who 'derive their strength from abuse of the legal process'. The judges also came down heavily on what it termed as 'calculated psychological offensives and mind games adopted to seek recusal of judges', which, it said, needed to 'be strongly repulsed'. 'We deprecate such tactics and recommend a similar approach to other courts when they experience such behaviour,' the court said.

To date, the Sahara group has been unable to raise Rs 10,000 crore to secure the bail of its jailed chief.

Impact

This landmark judgement is undoubtedly a milestone in India's corporate landscape as it sanctifies not only SEBI's absolute power to investigate into the matters of listed companies but also into the matters pertaining to the unlisted companies. It vests SEBI with myriad powers to investigate into any matter concerning the interest of the investors even if it pertains to companies which are not listed. It clarifies significant points of law and removes the grey areas relating to the issue of securities by the so-called unlisted companies taking advantage of the loopholes of the law. Also, in the matters of jurisdiction, this judgement has bridged the jurisdictional gap which previously existed between the Ministry of Corporate Affairs (MCA) and SEBI; it is hoped that in the future this judgement will be instrumental in preventing a turf war between the two with respect to jurisdictional issues, as the judgement categorically reiterates that in the matter of public interest, both SEBI and MCA will have concurrent jurisdiction. This is a welcome relief, as in the past, many defaulting parties have taken advantage of this jurisdictional lacuna and have been able to get off easily.

As mentioned before, the apex court, on 4 March 2014, sent Subrata Roy and two directors of his company to judicial custody till they paid another Rs 10,000 crore apart from the initial deposit of Rs 5120 crore. The fury of the court could be gauged from its order, which states that despite being given sufficient opportunities, there was no proposal to 'honour' its 31 August 2012 judgement and the subsequent orders of 5 December 2012 and 25 February 2013 to return the investors' money.

In the aftermath, the Supreme Court also ordered for a CBI probe into the massive funds collected by Saradha Chit Fund and other such companies in West Bengal, Orissa and Assam. So far, the federal probe agency has registered several cases against the culprits.

After the Sahara judgement, to protect the public from fraudulent money-pooling activities, SEBI has stepped up its action against entities raising funds illegally. This year alone, at least twenty-eight firms have faced SEBI's wrath for raising funds totalling to at least Rs 2500 crore through illegal money-pooling schemes or the unauthorized issuance of securities.

The action against these companies incidentally coincided with the recovery and attachment proceedings in recent months against hundreds of entities and those who had refused to pay their penalties and other dues to SEBI as per the capital market regulator's earlier orders.

The Securities Laws (Amendment) Act, 2014, has empowered SEBI to crack down on Ponzi schemes and investment frauds. The bill has given SEBI sweeping powers including the attachment of properties, launch of recovery proceedings, seeking call data records to investigate cases and ordering search and seizure against manipulators and fraudsters.

Sahara became the test case for the companies which had been launching such schemes and cheating gullible investors. Interestingly, between the time that SEBI first initiated the inquiry in 2009 and Roy's eventual arrest, there has not been a single instance of an investor—in either of the two Sahara firms under watch—actually filing a police complaint or going to court. In spite of SEBI's efforts of sending notices to lakhs of investors, a mere few hundreds came forward to claim their money.

The capital-market watchdog now has more powers such as carrying out search-and-seizure operations, clamping down on fraudsters and illegal money-pooling activities. After the Sahara judgement, SEBI has become more active and has begun to immediately initiate action on any companies resorting to such fraudulent schemes.

The government has enhanced the powers of SEBI to take action against illegal money-pooling activities valued at Rs 100 crore or more, and also providing for the setting up of a special court to expedite the cases filed by SEBI so that justice can be delivered to the public in a short time. SEBI has already taken action against entities that have collectively raised well above Rs 1 lakh crore through various schemes.

SEBI chairman, U.K. Sinha, has stated that agents, lured by 20–30 per cent commissions, have pushed illicit schemes among gullible investors in the absence of good savings products. The new efforts by the government to expand the financial inclusion of the common man will help curb the Ponzi menace in the country. States like West Bengal, Orissa, Bihar, Jharkhand and the ones in the North-East, where the penetration of banking services is low, have seen a larger number of people getting trapped in illegal money-pooling schemes that promise high returns.

New programmes like the Jan-Dhan Yojana scheme, launched by Prime Minister Narendra Modi to expand financial inclusion and banking coverage across the country, will help encourage people to put their money within a formal financial system. The Kisan Vikas Patra, in its new avatar, directly addresses the points to counter these fraudulent schemes. It offers a fixed return, such as being able to double the money in 100 months, relative ease of transaction without PAN registration and easy encashment after a two-and-a-half-year lock-in period, therefore succeeding in its objective of wooing the unbanked population of rural areas into having financial savings.

Winning Strokes

Arvind Datar, representing SEBI, argued that from the beginning both companies had planned to avoid SEBI involvement in the activities of the two companies. This was done with the sole purpose of having a free hand in their endeavours.

It is apparent from the declaration filed by these companies that reference to the Securities and Exchange Board of India Act, 1992 (the SEBI Act), to the rules made thereunder, as well as to the guidelines issued (by SEBI), as contained in the amended declaration, were omitted. The statutorily prescribed declaration was unilaterally and deliberately not adhered to by the two companies. This was done so that the companies could avoid SEBI's attention as well as wriggle out of the statutory requirements of the SEBI Act. The most significant violation and omission of the provisions of the SEBI Act was committed by asserting that invitation to the OFCDs was made by way of 'private placement', even though the aforesaid invitation was addressed to approximately 3 crore people, and was actually subscribed to by about 66 lakh investors. It was pointed out by Datar during the arguments that in case of an invitation to fifty or more people, the invitation is deemed to have been issued to the public.

In case of an offer or invitation to the public, an allotment of debentures can only be made through one or more recognized stock exchanges. Any allotment made in violation of the statutory provisions, as for instance, inviting a subscription in case of an issue 'to the public', without reference to a recognized stock exchange, is void. In such a situation, the Companies Act itself provides that the concerned company shall make a total refund of the money received by way of subscription. The subscription collected by these companies, which were admittedly to the tune of Rs 25,000 crore, is in complete violation of law, according to Datar.

The senior lawyer had argued that Sahara should be judged by what they actually did, not what they intended to do. He said that SIRECL and SHICL had pre-planned their affairs to avoid the involvement of SEBI in the activities of the two companies, so they could have a free hand in their endeavours.

In the declaration made by the two companies, they had clearly avoided references to SEBI and accordingly circumvented adherence to the provisions of the SEBI Act, rules and guidelines. The companies have likewise avoided the provisions of the Companies Act (which are under the administrative control of SEBI).

Since the subscription to the OFCDs under reference commenced in March 2008, the same raised suspicions about the genuineness and the bona fides of the companies. Surely, the suspicion was well placed. It was Arvind's contention that this itself was sufficient to conclude that the whole affair was doubtful, dubious and questionable. The contempt proceedings are still pending in the Supreme Court.

V

ARYAMA SUNDARAM:
TIRELESS GRIT

Born on 22 April 1957 in Chennai

To strive, to seek, to find, and not to yield.
—Lord Alfred Tennyson

IT WAS simply unbelievable, unimaginable and unthinkable. Can people ever be *this* callous? Can institutions ever be so indifferent? Can one's profession ever be deemed above humanity?

These thoughts weighed down on Aryama Sundaram's mind, all while he was patiently listening to the man in front of him. The man recollected and relived his traumatic experience with a sombre expression. But even as Sundaram—today, one of India's topmost lawyers—heard the painful tale, he kept thinking to himself: Why is he telling me all this? What does he expect from me?

When the gentleman finally finished his narrative, there was a stunned silence. The only thing Aryama didn't want to do was demean the man's purpose in life. The man narrating the heart-rending tale was international table-tennis champion V. Chandrashekhar.

Chandrashekhar was finding it difficult to piece together the traumatic experience he went through following his arthroscopic surgery at a very renowned hospital and the complications that arose thereafter. He was Aryama's classmate in Chennai, and the lawyer had often seen the ace table-tennis player in action, delivering his shots brilliantly, swinging his arm and then swinging it to the crowd in impeccable style. A shining table-tennis star, Chandrashekhar was a professional to the core. But at that time, he had been struggling to hold even a cup of coffee in his hands. His vision had been affected, and his hearing too. He was in such a critical condition and so upset that he wanted to sue the renowned hospital.

Chandrashekhar had approached Sundaram six months after his surgery with a definite purpose in mind. Chandrashekhar was twenty-five then and had undergone a minor surgery for a knee injury in 1984. The surgery had gone wrong and he had been plunged into a near-coma state over the period of a month.

What transpired after this would be one of Sundaram's career highlights as well as one of the biggest and most controversial cases to rock the country. It was a medical malpractice suit, one of the first of its kind in 1986. In fact, the case was filed and fought at a time when there was no kind of consumer-protection law available, and when even the Consumer Protection Act, 1986, as we know it today, wasn't in existence. 'My client wanted compensation. I took up the case and filed the first medical malpractice suit in India against a reputed hospital for negligence,' Sundaram reminisces.

The lawsuit was filed in 1986. The trial lasted more than five years. It was in 1993 that Chandrashekhar was awarded around Rs 17.38 lakh as compensation, along with interest, a total sum of Rs 31 lakh in all. This was an unbelievable amount to receive in a compensation case in India. Though the hospital appealed before the Madras High Court, the matter went to the Supreme Court and, finally, the hospital settled the matter after arriving at a mutually agreeable figure with Chandrashekhar. The trial made headlines, and for Sundaram, it was a huge personal success.

'I can never forget this case . . . this period of my life. I am still in touch with Chandrashekhar and the table-tennis academy.

Chandrashekhar's life has turned around for the better. Perhaps, it was a turning point for both of us,' Sundaram muses.

Why I Became a Lawyer

Sundaram belonged to an old, traditional family in Tamil Nadu, one that had produced lawyers over five generations. However, when Sundaram began his practice, funnily enough, he was the only lawyer in the family. His father, C.R. Sundaram, had retired as the chairman of the National Small Industries Corporation, a public sector enterprise.

Aryama's grandfather, C.P. Ramaswamy Aiyar, aka Sir C.P., was a renowned lawyer. He was very particular that Sundaram join the legal profession. Unfortunately, he died when Sundaram was just nine. His grandfather had been keen on his grandson continuing the family tradition of becoming a lawyer. As none of his other grandchildren showed any inclination towards the law, Sir C.P.'s interest in Sundaram, who was also the youngest of the lot, grew.

'I remember when he was leaving for England; he made it very clear to the family about my becoming a lawyer. In those days, he had the privilege of boarding the plane separately, with his car driven to the aircraft. I accompanied him to the airport to have a look at the aircraft. He was so fond of me that he took me inside the plane. He wanted me to see what the aircraft was like from the inside.

Sir C.P. would constantly seek reassurance from the young Sundaram that he would follow the profession of a lawyer; the young boy would unfailingly adhere to his grandfather's words. Even on the day Sundaram accompanied him into the aircraft for a dekko, his grandfather asked him about his future aspirations. 'I could see his smile grow bigger as soon as I reassured him with

my answer that I too wanted to become a lawyer . . . and in the
next moment, he hugged me. That was the last hug, the last smile
I ever saw. My grandfather never returned home. He passed away
in London,' Sundaram says.

What Sir C.P. said, however, always reverberated with
Sundaram, and he took it upon himself to fulfil his last wish—of
Sundaram becoming a lawyer. His uncle C.R. Pattabhiraman too
was a renowned lawyer and went on to become the law minister
in Indira Gandhi's government in the 1960s. He had stopped his
practice in the 1970s, much before Sundaram himself enrolled
as a lawyer.

Sundaram completed his schooling from the Lawrence School,
Lovedale. He graduated in 1976 from Vivekananda College,
Chennai, and was a gold medallist in philosophy. 'You should
rank first,' his mother, Kamakshi Sundaram, a medical doctor by
profession, would always insist. 'My mother would ensure that
I studied till late, especially during my final exams,' Sundaram
says about the hard work he was expected to put in to fulfil the
high expectations his parents had. But his father would always
be sympathetic towards his son. He would often find Sundaram
awake late and studying in his room and tell the young boy,
'Don't stress. Go to sleep now.'

'I was not even aware of what stress meant, but I was quite
conscious of my studies and would allow my mother to have her
way. Her words, "You have to come first," would always echo in
my ears,' Sundaram says.

Aryama had once taken part in an elocution competition
at the age of seven and had come in second, having lost by one
point to the eventual winner. When he entered his house with
the trophy, his mother rushed towards him with great delight and
said, 'Congratulations on your win!' But when he told her that he
had in fact won the second position in the contest, and that the

student who came first had received a bigger trophy, his mother berated him, saying, 'A little more . . . how little more? A little less is worlds apart.' Sundaram says, 'I think from then on I kept trying to do that little bit more.'

Sundaram was always a good debater. In fact, he would debate in college, often representing the university he was a part of, and won the top position on several occasions. 'I was fond of dramatics too. I used to participate in plays and would often go for rehearsals after work. I have also directed a few plays. Theatre was a passion for me. In sports, I was very keen on golf and regularly played table tennis and cricket. I was also fond of horse riding,' he says.

Sundaram earned his law degree from the Madras Law College. It was only after finishing his degree there that he realized that in hindsight, he had never aspired to become anything else. But he was keen on trying his hands at a new field. 'I think it was right to introspect at this point of time in life. It helped me to take up a job in an advertising agency. I joined the reputed Ogilvy & Mather [O&M] advertising agency as a part of the client services department [marketing]. I worked there for a year and a half.'

Despite his academic training as a lawyer, Sundaram took a great shine to advertising and wanted to make a career of it. He was, in fact, earning a handsome salary as an accounts executive and even had his own car back then. 'Son, you are a lawyer. Why don't you try and start your law practice?' said his father one day.

In those days, lawyers were not paid so well. They would earn a paltry sum. Sundaram was young and was already earning a good income from his advertising job. Why should I go into law? he questioned himself, and made his father understand the financial repercussions. He was convinced that he was not going to earn anything as a lawyer.

Sundaram's father had retired by then. However, he had never forced his son into returning to the law. 'You will have some income in a month . . . if you want to go into law,' said his father one day to him. Earning money was certainly not a condition for Sundaram to take up the law, but his father wanted the young man to be independent and have his own practice. His father was even willing to rent out property he owned to help his son out and provide him with some assured monthly income and start his own practice.

'The idea of being independent appealed to me. It was a fair bargain, and I decided to try it out. If I didn't like it, I thought I could always come back to advertising. It was this back-up plan that made me take the risk,' Sundaram said.

King & Partridge

After leaving O&M, Sundaram enrolled with the Madras Bar Council on 26 November 1980, and joined a law firm called King & Partridge. At the time, it was an old but prominent (formerly British) firm in Chennai, with offices in Bangalore, and associates in Kolkata and New Delhi. The firm did its own litigation work.

'The day I joined, I got some litigation work. I was very interested in litigation. My first day in office was filled with excitement that I was actually—finally—a lawyer. I was very fortunate that in my very first week I was asked to go to the court for an adjournment because my senior was not around. What I liked and appreciated the most was the system of being thoroughly familiar with the case before going to the court, even for an adjournment or while asking for a passover,' Sundaram said.

This early training and tuning-in to read every case that he was concerned with contributed a lot to Sundaram becoming a successful lawyer. He got into the habit of reading every single case before going to court. The firm had a lot of cases to deal with. As a routine, every morning, the clerk would go around handing over to every junior lawyer his or her share of the four or five cases to be taken up for formal fixing of dates or an adjournment. There were about thirty to forty cases that were dealt with every day by the firm.

The lawyers who were drawing a fixed salary would usually be reluctant to go to court. However, Sundaram had a very different approach. He was very flexible and would ask the clerk to give him any number of cases. Sundaram's only request was for him to get the briefs at least one hour before the scheduled hearing, so that he could go through the issues and segregate them and be fully prepared even when asking for adjournments and passovers.

It was important to him that he always be ready with the brief. His dedication and commitment soon brought in rich dividends. 'I had not even completed three months when two senior people, V. Aravamudan, a leading shipping expert, and S. Ramasubramanian, my senior and mentor in the firm, noticed and complimented me and acknowledged the interest I showed in my work,' Sundaram remembers proudly.

His Senior

Ramasubramanian was the senior Sundaram worked with. He was very sharp and never repeated instructions. He would always come straight to the point, being a very busy man. Since Ramasubramanian travelled a lot, Sundaram would have to go to court and keep seeking adjournments very often. Sometimes, these would not be granted and he ended up arguing many cases, rather unusual for a junior with less than a year at the Bar.

'I used to be prepared and would happily go ahead with the case. I must say I was very young, not even six months into the profession, when I regularly started going to the Madras High Court,' he says.

His First Great Experience

Sundaram's first big case was in 1981, when Aravamudan asked him to attend to an appeal related to earnest money in the High Court. Earnest money is a deposit made to a seller to confirm a contract, and is often used in real-estate transactions.

Justice Suryamurthi was known to be a very tough judge and most lawyers were scared of him. He was scheduled to preside over the case, and Sundaram was advised by Aravamudan to remember that the judge loved literature and good English.

'When the case was called, I told the judge, "My Lord, this case is about the importance of being earnest, and I am not referring to the play by Oscar Wilde. The judge immediately started laughing and encouraged me greatly in my arguments thereafter. I must have argued the case for a day and a half—and I won it,' Aryama says proudly.

The case instilled in him the much-required confidence needed to excel in the big league. After this, for any case, he became the obvious choice for matters before Justice Suryamurthi.

When Sundaram joined King & Partridge, he worked without a salary in the beginning. All he was offered in return were two cups of coffee without sugar. 'I had proved my merit, and my senior, Ramasubramanian, started assigning more and more work to me,' he says. Though he was not allowed to privately practise, after about a year and a half Sundaram was offered a position at a retainership of Rs 350 per month. Within a year, his salary increased threefold. And in just three and a half years, he became one of the highest-paid lawyers in the firm.

In 1984, during the summer holidays, some of the lawyers in King & Partridge decided to start their own practice. They left the firm and wanted Sundaram to join them. It was a difficult decision for Sundaram, since his wife and he were expecting their first child soon, and to give up the salary that his job at King & Partridge brought him and to take the risk of private practice was not easy. However, Sundaram was fully supported by his wife in making this decision. 'Even I wanted to start my own practice. So we started our own firm: Nataraj Rao Raghu & Sundaram. In Madras, Mumbai and Calcutta, there is tremendous scope for original-side practice. Our firm became one of the leading firms in handling commercial, shipping and property cases,' he says.

In the due course of time, Sundaram became the leading admiralty lawyer in the Madras High Court. He would do all the litigation himself. 'In our firm, we were five partners, and I was the youngest. We were a happy lot. We never had arguments. When we started out, we would all sit in one room. When the firm became bigger, we still continued to sit in one room. Gradually, the firm got bigger and bigger, and we had to take the entire floor of the building. My partners are still there, but I moved on,' he says.

In 1989, Sundaram's firm was dealing with a case that they had lost in the Madras High Court. It was a significant case in India on the issue of freedom of speech. 'We came to the Supreme Court, and I briefed senior counsel Soli Sorabjee. Mukul Mudgal, who later became the Chief Justice of the Punjab and Haryana High Court, was the advocate on record, and I was the briefing counsel. Ever since that case, I have been a huge believer in the freedom of speech,' Sundaram says.

The specifics of this landmark case on the freedom of speech and expression, *S. Rangarajan v. P. Jagjivan Ram* (judgement delivered on 30 March 1989), are that Rangarajan had produced a Tamil film *Ore Oru Gramathile* and applied for a certificate for the exhibition of the film. The examination committee had refused to grant the certificate, but on a reference being made to the second revising committee for review and recommendation, the committee, by a majority of 5:4, recommended a 'U' certificate, subject to the deletion of certain scenes. The granting of the certificate was challenged at the High Court on the ground that the film had been treated in an irresponsible manner, that the reservation policy of the government had been projected in a biased manner and that the so-called appeal of the film that 'India is One' was hollow and sensationalist, touching sensitive caste matters. It was also asserted that the film would create law and order problems in Tamil Nadu. The High Court ultimately revoked the certificate and banned the film.

Two appeals, one by the producer of the film and the other by the Union of India were filed at the Supreme Court. The issue of the breach of law and order and violence was raised by the state of Tamil Nadu regarding the exhibition of the film. The Supreme Court firmly rejected the state's plea, stating: 'Freedom of expression cannot be suppressed on account of threat of demonstration and processions or threats of violence. That would tantamount to negation of the rule of law and a surrender to blackmail and intimidation.' The apex court reiterated: 'It is the duty of the State to protect freedom of expression. The State cannot plead its inability to handle the hostile audience problem. It is its obligatory duty to prevent it and protect the freedom of expression.' It is noteworthy that the Supreme Court endorsed the celebrated dictum of the European Court of Human Rights that freedom of expression guarantees 'not only views that are generally received but also those that offend, shock or disturb the State or any sector of the population. Such are the demands of that pluralism, tolerance and broadmindedness without which there is no democratic society'.

Within three and a half years of his enrolment as a lawyer, Sundaram was shortlisted by a big corporate group to give his opinion on a complicated issue on trust law. Simultaneously, the managing director of the company had also referred the matter to the then Attorney General of India. Sundaram was, however, asked to reconsider his opinion as it was contrary to the one given by the top law officer. The young lawyer refused to budge and, ultimately, the company ended up following the course that Sundaram had suggested. After this, the corporate group treated him as their main legal adviser and referred all their legal matters to him. But for Sundaram, this was a turning point in his professional career as it taught him to have the courage and conviction to believe and act on his beliefs and what he felt was correct. It also taught him how to think originally and not follow a path merely because it had been followed before or was believed to be the best course of action by anyone else—even the numero uno lawyer of India.

'When Soli Sorabjee became the Attorney General for the first time in 1989, he wanted me to become the central government's standing counsel. I was doing well in my firm, but I took up the offer as I felt there was no impediment in my practice as I was allowed to carry on with my private practice. I continued with this post for six years till I got designated as a senior counsel in 1995. During this period, I would travel frequently to other High Courts to conduct admiralty cases,' Sundaram says.

Becoming a Senior

In the Madras High Court, the rule was that a lawyer had to be at least forty-five years of age to be designated as a senior advocate; in special cases, this condition could be waived if s/he had clocked fifteen years of practice. Sundaram became a senior within fifteen years of his enrolment. He was thirty-eight at the time—the youngest ever to be designated as a senior in the history of the Madras High Court.

In those days, one did not apply to be a senior counsel. The usual practice was that two seniors would send a proposal to the Chief Justice, after which the registrar of the concerned High Court would ask for the consent of the concerned lawyer. After receiving consent, a full court would sit, discuss and decide whether to make someone a senior or not.

It was Chennai-based senior lawyer Govind Swaminadhan who took the initiative and was instrumental in Sundaram being designated as a senior. He drafted his proposal. 'Swaminadhan was an absolutely phenomenal man . . . Honest to the core. It was during my tenure at King & Partridge that I got to work with him often,' says Sundaram. The firm would often use his services and brief him on several occasions. His fondest memories of Swaminadhan was that he was a keen horseman and got Sundaram to start riding—the two of them would ride every morning at 5.30 a.m.

'I was on a flight to New Delhi for a case coming up in the Supreme Court that evening, when the notification of my being designated as a senior counsel was received at my chambers. My advocate on record, Mukul Mudgal, who later became the Chief Justice of the Punjab and Haryana High Court, was informed by my colleagues, and when I landed in Delhi and went to see him, he greeted me with a gift of my first "senior robes". He then informed me that he had called off the planned conference with the senior who was proposed to be briefed in the matter by me—on the basis that there was now anyway a senior for the case. And so my first case as a senior lawyer was before the Supreme Court the next morning—and I succeeded,' says Sundaram with pride.

After spending six years as a senior counsel in the Madras High Court, he decided to move to Delhi.

Relocating to Delhi

In Delhi, Sundaram came in contact with a lot of new people. He believes that it is extremely important for any person of any profession, especially a lawyer, to have a wide exposure to the world. 'When you are dealing with a profession like law, then your exposure counts a lot and determines how you will be able to handle your cases. Your exposure to the world comes from meeting different people from different nationalities and cultures and, above all, different economic strata,' he says.

Sundaram has always been very social. He has a lot of friends, and they often meet over the weekends. 'I enjoy socializing because I get to learn a lot. I get to socialize whether I go to watch a Formula One race, or go watch a golf tournament. I do not, however, socialize for the sake of socializing. I do so when I feel I'm going to enjoy myself doing it,' he says.

Most people, when they move to Delhi, go as 'law officers'. As a law officer, one gets the adequate exposure in the professional sense and can even think of starting a private practice. Sundaram, however, moved to set up not only his house but also his office. 'I was not a law officer and I did not have any fixed practice. For the first two to three months, things were too slow in Delhi compared to what I was doing in Chennai. And when I did not have any cases on a given day, I would fly to Chennai because I always had cases there,' he says.

'Sundaram, have you moved to Delhi?' asked eminent lawyer G.L. Sanghi one day, who had tried on several occasions to refer some cases to him, but each time Sundaram happened to be in Chennai.

'Whenever I am free here and there is no case in Delhi, then I leave for Chennai,' Sundaram replied.

'If you have moved here, then don't go back to Chennai,' Sanghi said, further advising Sundaram to keep himself busy with either reading books or other things.

'They keep calling me every day to Chennai. I have so many cases to handle there,' Sundaram told him.

'This won't help you settle down. When I moved here, Chandigarh would keep calling me. Even if you are willing to leave your parent court, your parent court is not really willing to leave you,' Sanghi said to Sundaram. He continued, 'It becomes difficult to resist and then one day I made a rule for myself that I would go to any other court in India, but I won't visit the Punjab and Haryana High Court for one year.'

Sanghi advised Sundaram to accept cases anywhere he desired, but not to go to the Madras High Court. Sundaram followed his advice. For six months, he did not take up a single case in the Madras High Court except for some briefings and found himself getting correspondingly very busy in Delhi.

'I must say that when I moved here, I found Delhi to be the least parochial city of all. Today, a lot of cases I appear in come from Delhi, Mumbai and Gujarat—a lot more than from Chennai,' Sundaram says.

When he finally moved to Delhi, he was very keen for his mother to join him there. But this did not materialize. 'She is deeply rooted to her own place. I am quite attached to her, and this makes me travel to Chennai quite often. My family is in Chennai, and my children, Skanda, Madhulika, and daughter-in-law, Nivruti, are working there, with no intentions of moving to Delhi,' Sundaram says.

On 15 May 2014, Sundaram's mother celebrated her ninetieth birthday. A doctor, she started the New Delhi Family Planning Association. Those days his parents lived in Delhi. When his father retired, they moved to South India. Sundaram was eleven years old then.

'My mother was a storehouse of ideas. She would often think about new schemes, new ideas—how to do the same things in new and different ways. She is the one who taught me how to think . . . how to think originally. She has been a major influence on my way of thinking,' he says.

His mother was a great inspiration to Sundaram, of course, but he gets all his gentlemanly qualities from his father. Sundaram's father was a complete gentleman, someone who was very soft-spoken and never ever had a bad word to say against anyone.

'My father would often say, "There is so much that is good in the worst of us . . . and so much that is bad in the best of us . . . It little behoves some of us to talk ill of the rest of us." I still follow his sage advice and even tell others about it,' says Sundaram.

Sundaram's professional career has greatly been influenced by the kind of qualities his parents have instilled in him. All this, according to him, has helped him to have an unbiased approach towards his client and cases.

His Daily Routine

'My day begins at 8.30 a.m. and ends at around 10 p.m. I have no breaks in between. I sleep late, and wake up late, around 7.30 a.m. I sleep only six hours. Then I read the newspapers. Usually, I have some conferences to attend in the morning and then I leave for court. After finishing my court work, I exercise till 6 p.m., followed by evening conferences which go on till I am adequately prepared for all cases. I often give my views on panels and discussions on various news channels on various current issues of national importance. Thereafter, I watch some TV and do some revision for my cases and sleep fairly late,' Sundaram says.

From the day he joined the profession, he would take one day off every week. He never works on Sundays and also makes time for vacations. When he became a senior counsel, he decided not to appear before vacation courts. This, in fact, was advised to him by Swaminadhan.

'I still don't work during vacations. I have only two exceptions to this rule—one, if it is a case that I have already argued in the High Court and which has come up in the Supreme Court and is urgent; and two, if I have got an order in the Supreme Court, and the other side has moved for any modification of the order. Otherwise, I don't take up cases during the vacations,' Sundaram says.

He has consciously decided to not take on more than seven special leave petitions (SLPs) in a day. 'Today, most get cases that require heavy briefing and detailed study. Accordingly, the arguments may even be longer and more discussion-oriented, and one cannot simply argue a case in just ten seconds. And if you use your time judiciously, then you cannot do justice to more than five to seven cases a day,' he says.

Sundaram has been representing the BCCI in a number of cases for quite some time. Currently, he is handling the infamous Indian Premier League (IPL) spot-fixing and betting case being heard at the Supreme Court.

In January, earlier this year, the Supreme Court barred N. Srinivasan, the beleaguered BCCI president from contesting any BCCI elections on the grounds of conflict of interest. A judges' committee was set up to decide on the penalty. It held that there was a conflict of interest by virtue of Srinivasan being the BCCI chief *and* owning an IPL franchisee, the Chennai Super Kings (CSK), through Indian Cements, a company he manages. It was further held that the allegation of betting against Gurunath Meiyappan, a CSK team official who happens to be the son-in-law of Srinivasan, and Rajasthan Royals co-owner Raj Kundra, stands proved while the charge of a cover-up against Srinivasan 'is not proved and at best there's only a case of suspicion against Srinivasan of a cover-up'. The apex court had appointed a three-member committee to conduct an independent inquiry into the allegations of corruption against Meiyappan, India Cements and the Rajasthan Royals team owner, Jaipur IPL Cricket Private Ltd, as well as allegations around betting and spot-fixing in IPL matches and the involvement of players. It was also held that not only players and team officials but 'franchisees will also be punished for misconduct'. The future of CSK and IPL could be in danger as IPL rules provide for the cancellation of the franchise for misconduct by players, owners and officials of a team.

Sundaram represented the industry association, the Federation of Indian Chambers of Commerce and Industry (FICCI), in the 2G spectrum presidential reference, which was moved by the UPA government in the backdrop of the apex court judgement cancelling all 122 2G spectrum licences, and seeking clarification on the mode of allocation of natural resources by the government. In this case, a five-judge bench presided over by the then Chief Justice of India S.H. Kapadia held that the auction was a preferable method for the allotment of natural resources, but that it could not be said to be the only method for allocating all natural resources by the government.

Sundaram has also appeared for the West Bengal government against The Chatterjee Group (TCG), with the court upholding the government's refusal to transfer shares to the group. Subsequently, the Supreme Court, in another round of litigation in 2013, allowed TCG to go ahead in the International Court of Arbitration in France to settle its dispute over the sale of up to 155 million shares of Haldia Petrochemicals Ltd.

A Perfect Lawyer

A perfect lawyer is one who has the ability to think. S/he should have the confidence and the ability to think originally. An ideal lawyer should have the courage to be able to voice and state what s/he believes in, and should possess integrity as a person and a legal professional. And that should make him or her a role model. S/he should have the ability to communicate most effectively in the shortest possible time and the shortest possible way.

On being asked as to whether he considers himself arrogant, Sundaram says, 'There are some who feel that I am arrogant, and they may have their own reasons. All those who have worked with me or have ever been associated with me in any way have never felt any arrogance from me creeping into our interactions.'

'I guess there is a very thin line that separates the fine distinction between an ideal lawyer, a perfect lawyer and a good lawyer. There is a great deal of subjectivity in this demarcation,' he continued. 'At the end of the day what really matters is one's sincere approach to the task at hand, and the knowledge that s/he has done his/her best,' says Sundaram. 'One thing I would certainly like to stress upon is that a lawyer should not take up cases if they cannot handle it or do justice to it. It is important to have a disciplined code of conduct and a code of practice. It is equally important that when you take up a case for a client, you have to be totally loyal to him/her.'

'Facts will be facts, and I feel it's important to give due respect to facts, whether they are in your favour or against you. More importantly, if there is case law is against you, then it becomes your duty to place the case before the court and then deal with it,' he says.

Sundaram's most regret-worthy moment was pursuing the Sahara case—his advice and course of action was not followed on three occasions. On the third such occasion, he withdrew from the case—the first time he ever did so. 'I feel all lawyers should be very sensitive to the fact that when they are arguing a case, they should make it a point to bring all the facts to the notice of the court,' he says.

'My vision—or, rather, my hope—is that the next-generation lawyer should be in a position to avail of all the advantages available in this techno-savvy society, with its myriad ways to access information. However, at the same time, s/he should follow the fundamental quality of a lawyer to deeply research cases and read a good number of law books, cases and other literature to improve his/her knowledge. This is absolutely essential as they go further in their profession,' he says. 'The modern lawyer should not forget that law was called a "learned profession" because the lawyer was meant to be a learned man, not only with regard to the laws but also with regard to life and society in general—be it literature, philosophy and theology—and that quality becomes more and more important as one progresses in the profession,' Sundaram sums up.

His Approach

When Sundaram takes up a case, he studies it completely. 'If and when I take up a case, then 95 per cent chances are that I will be there for it, and that speaks for my reputation. When I am briefed, I will be present for the matter for sure, and I think it is important because that's the only way your client will have faith in you . . . You can't let him/her down. I see no logic in preparing for twenty cases and then just appearing in ten,' he says.

Sundaram doesn't charge a penny for a hearing that he is not able to get to the court in time for. He does take an advance fee, which he returns in case he can't make it to the hearings. 'My chamber is very clear that the cheque should be issued on the spot and be handed over to my clerk. That is a standing rule. I feel that you don't have any right to take the fees when you have not appeared,' he says.

Sundaram also does many cases pro bono. 'If I am convinced that the causes for which people are fighting are genuine, then I do such cases free of cost. If someone is fighting a commercial issue, then the question of doing the matter for free does not arise. For people I know, friends of mine, I would never charge any fees,' he says.

Hall of Legal Fame

Aryama Sundaram's strength is rooted in his willingness and ability to think originally. His courage, conviction and integrity make him stand apart. He is one of the top lawyers to be picked for arguing complex corporate matters.

Apart from being a persuasive speaker, he appreciates and respects people on an equal level. He hardly loses his cool and has good oratory skills. He has his own views. Loyalty is an important characteristic that he looks for people.

He loves travelling during court vacations. 'I go all over the world. I have a house in Kodaikanal that I keep visiting. I love Goa too. I have a family house in Ooty as well. I take my holidays seriously.'

Sundaram also enjoys watching all forms of dance, listening to all genres of music and watching movies. His choice of music is opera. 'When I look back, I believe I have led a full and satisfying life, both professionally and otherwise. I do not, therefore, believe in rewinding the clock since it would mean doing the same things all over again. I would rather look at the present, at what I am doing and, perhaps, look ahead at what I would like to do,' he says.

Rohini Musa, a lawyer associated with Sundaram's chamber for more than a decade, says: 'Every junior lawyer should get the opportunity to be associated with Mr Sundaram and his chambers. There is only one senior whom you will look up to as your mentor, who instils in you the prized values of integrity and grit, who enjoys an honest debate, who does not ridicule an original thought, whose pride knows no bounds at your successes, who can inspire awe in you and yet make you laugh at a joke cracked by him—that is Mr Sundaram. There is none other like him.'

'These six years assisting Mr Sundaram have been quite satisfying. Though he encourages us a lot, he expects his juniors to go through every minute detail in a matter. He gives us the freedom to argue in the courts and is always there to hand-hold us. I could not have asked for any other senior who is as accessible as him,' says Zafar Inayat, a lawyer who works in Sundaram's chamber.

To sum up, Sundaram cites a few lines from 'If', a poem by Rudyard Kipling: 'If you can fill the unforgiving minute/With sixty seconds' worth of distance run/Yours is the Earth and everything that's in it/And—which is more—you'll be a Man, my son!'

THE CASE

Sterlite Industries (I) Ltd v. Union of India
Judgement delivered by bench comprising Justices A.K. Patnaik and H.L. Gokhale on 2 April 2013

Case Details

For upholding the law, courts are often required to strike a fine balance between two seemingly rightful but contrasting positions. The Supreme Court judgement on the dispute over industrial development and ecological preservation between Sterlite Industries and the residents in a Tamil Nadu village is a fine example.

Throwing out arguments seeking the permanent closure of the copper-smelting plant of Sterlite, a unit of the London-listed NRI billionaire Anil Aggarwal–led Vedanta Resources Plc, the apex court slapped a hefty penalty of

Rs 100 crore on Sterlite for flouting environmental laws for a period of over five years.

The Sterlite plant, one of the leading copper-smelting plants in the world, is located in an ecologically fragile coastal area in Meelavittan village, Tuticorin, a port city in Tamil Nadu. It may be noted that the islands between the Tuticorin and Rameswaram shores in the Gulf of Mannar were notified as the first marine biosphere reserve of India.

Four such islands—Vanthivu, Kasuwar, Karaichalli and Villanguchalli—are all within a short distance of Tuticorin, where the copper-smelting plant is located.

Upholding the polluter-pays principle, the apex court sent a strong signal, saying, 'Any less amount would not have the desired deterrent effect on the company,' and the amount of compensation should be decided on the basis of the financial strength of the company.

Sterlite had obtained all the necessary clearances from the Ministry of Environment and Forests and the Tamil Nadu Pollution Control Board (TNPCB) between 1994–95 for the setting up of the plant. However, these consent orders under the air and water laws granted by the authorities came under challenge before the Madras High Court. While the writ petitions were pending, the company went ahead and commenced production in January 1997.

Soon, V. Gopalsamy, general secretary of the regional political outfit MDMK, Thayagam and K. Kanagaraj, secretary of the CITU district committee in Tuticorin, and others, sought court directives against the company to stop operations at the plant, and against the government for its failure to check pollution. They also demanded safety measures to avoid industrial accidents.

Petitions by them alleged that the company was running the unit without any mandatory clearances and in violation of green norms, causing damage to the environment and public health.

A decade later, the High Court dealt a fatal blow on 28 September 2010 by asking the company to close down its plant for failing to comply with environmental norms and also directed it to compensate the employees. It also wanted the state government to re-employ the workforce in some other companies so as to protect their livelihood.

Aggrieved by the High Court order, Sterlite moved the Supreme Court. While the matter was pending, a fresh row over a 'toxic' gas leak from the plant on 27 March 2013 surfaced. The TNPCB shut the plant down within two days.

While setting aside the Madras High Court's judgement, the apex court fined Sterlite $20 million (Rs 100 crore on conversion into rupees on the then prevailing exchange rate of Rs 50 for a dollar) for over-pollution from its huge copper smelter.

The company was asked to deposit the money with the Thoothukudi district collector. The amount was to be kept in a fixed deposit in a nationalized bank for a minimum period of five years, renewable as and when it expired, and the interest from it was to be spent on improving the environment, including water and soil quality, of the vicinity of the plant that had been affected adversely over the years. Sterlite Industries had been operating its copper-smelter plant between 1997 and 2012. The Supreme Court also imposed a heavy fine, stating: 'Compensation must act as a deterrent, and any amount less than Rs 100 crore would not have the desired impact.'

The apex court held Sterlite guilty of pollution and breach of environmental standards and, later, of running the unit without consent orders after the state authorities withdrew its clearances for causing harm to the plant's surroundings.

While the court noted that the company had suppressed facts by claiming it ran the plant with statutory consents, it refused to direct closure, saying the plant contributed substantially to copper production and generated a large revenue for the government.

Sterlite was relieved that the shutdown order was negated, but the Supreme Court did not prevent the state authorities from taking action against the company's environmental lapses, with closure not ruled out as a punitive measure. Sterlite promised to 'fully cooperate' with the authorities.

What weighed heavy in favour of Sterlite is that the plant contributed substantially to the copper production in India, and copper is used in defence, electricity, automobile, construction and infrastructure, etc. 'The plant of the appellants has about 1300 employees and it also provides employment to a large number of people through contractors. A number of ancillary industries are also dependent on the plant. Through its various transactions, the plant generates a huge revenue for the central and state governments in terms of excise, custom duties, income tax and VAT. It also contributes to 10 per cent of the total cargo volume of Tuticorin port. For these considerations of public interest, we do not think it will be a proper exercise of our discretion under Article 136 of the Constitution to refuse relief on the grounds of misrepresentation and suppression of material facts in the special leave petition,' the apex court observed.

Impact

In consonance with the principle of sustainable development, the Supreme Court struck a fine balance between industrial development and ecological preservation. The judgement sent a stern message to companies that doing business in a socially and environmentally responsible manner is more than just a legal obligation, and there is a need to strike the right balance.

The gas leak from Sterilite's plant reminds us of the December 1984 leak of the deadly methyl isocyanate gas from a Union Carbide plant in Bhopal, which exposed over 5,00,000 people to the toxic gas, killing around 3800 people and maiming several thousands. Lessons have been learnt. Companies now have to be ready to pay the heavy price for the violation of environmental norms.

'Heavy compensation costs co-related to the magnitude and capacity of the enterprise should be imposed, as such compensation may have a deterrent effect, and the larger and more prosperous the enterprise, the greater must be the amount of compensation payable by it,' the Supreme Court observed in its order.

While Sterilite had been operating the plant in the area since 1995, and contributing significantly to the country's production of the metal, residents feel that the copper smelter was the biggest polluter in the region. Fishermen blame discharging of untreated waste water into the sea for the reduced catch.

The National Green Tribunal has been set up to look into the issues of environmental degradation as such instances have gone up in the past few years. With the courts taking up such cases, the voluntary bodies too are feeling encouraged to come forward to take up the cause of the environment in the interest of the public at large, particularly against the mighty and the resourceful. It's this combined effort which may help to mitigate this potent threat.

Government authorities are expected to be objective in their approach and should strive to make the process of giving environmental clearances more comprehensive, predictable and transparent.

Winning Arguments

Senior counsel Sundaram, who himself hails from Tamil Nadu, tore apart the High Court judgement, saying that none of the grounds which formed the basis for directing closure of the plant were well-founded. He submitted that the plant produced 2,02,000 metric tonnes of copper, which constitutes 39 per cent of the total of 5,14,000 metric tonnes of copper produced in India, and that 50 per cent of the copper produced by the plant is consumed in the domestic market and the balance 50 per cent is exported abroad. The plant provides direct and indirect employment to about 3000 people and yields a huge revenue to both the central and state governments, and that the closure of the plant would not be in public interest.

Sundaram denied reports that the Sterlite plant had caused severe pollution in the area and contaminated the groundwater, thus making it unfit for consumption. He was forceful in his submissions that the recommendations given by the TNPCB were only to provide the best of checks in the plant against environmental pollution so as to ensure that the plant becomes a model plant from the environment's point of view, but that that did not mean the plant had deficiencies which needed to be corrected.

He contended that while the reports of the National Environmental Engineering and Research Institute (NEERI) referred to the accumulation of gypsum and phosphogypsum which come out from the plant as part of the slag, the pollution control boards opined that such slag was non-hazardous and could be used in cement industries for filling up lower-lying areas and as building/road construction material, etc., and had no adverse environmental effects. Besides, according to Sundaram, the Rapid Environment Impact Assessment, before granting clearance to the plant, was conducted in accordance with the guidelines.

The High Court—having noticed some decisions of the apex court on sustainable development, namely, the precautionary and polluter-pays principles, and the public trust doctrine—had failed to appreciate that the decision of the central government to grant environmental clearance to the plant could only be tested on the anvil of well-recognized principles of judicial review.

In the absence of a mandatory requirement in the procedure laid down in the scheme under the Environment (Protection) Act, 1986, at the relevant time, of requiring a mandatory public hearing and a mandatory comprehensive environmental impact assessment report, the High Court could not have interfered with the decision of the central government to grant environmental clearance on the grounds of procedural impropriety.

The TNPCB had considered the representation of the company and permitted it to reduce the width of the green belt from 250 metres to 25 metres around the battery limit of the industry, and there was nothing to show that this exercise of power was vitiated by irrationality or procedural breach or any breach of the mandatory provisions of the law, thus the High Court could not have interfered with the exercise of such power by the state pollution control board, Sundaram had pointed out.

VI

PRASHANT BHUSHAN: A LEGAL ACTIVIST

Born on 15 October 1956 in Allahabad

To do great things, you don't necessarily need a grand plan. Even with one step at a time, and public interest in mind, you can still make a significant impact.
—Prashant Bhushan

SOMETHING WAS definitely wrong. He was brushed aside by security personnel who were rushing towards the entry point. In the ensuing uproar the only thing audible was, *'Pakda gaya saala!'* ['The scoundrel has been caught!']

Prashant was caught unawares by the commotion outside Court Number 5 at the Allahabad High Court while he was on his way towards Court Number 24 to witness the historic proceedings that were to shortly begin. A burly, shabby man was whisked away by the security men and, soon, the hullabaloo subsided.

Prashant's curiosity aroused, he decided to figure out what had caused the sudden flux of activity. 'What happened?' he asked an elderly gentleman who was blissfully unaware of what had just ensued despite being near the place of the incident. Had it not been for the metal detector and an alert security system, a man carrying a loaded country-made pistol in a plastic briefcase would have conveniently made it inside the court premises on the day the Prime Minister of India was to be cross-examined.

Prashant remembers thinking to himself then, going by how the day started and what one could expect to ensue—what with the country's most important political figures to be questioned—that the day already had the makings of an unforgettable one! The stakes couldn't be higher!

Given the imminent arrival of the nation's prime minister, the security was understandably very stringent, and there was no room for any kind of desirable or undesirable theatricality. 'I was born into a lawyer's family and was well-versed with the routine procedures and conventions, especially those involving the mundane and sometimes extremely boring cross-examinations. But that day was nothing like any other day . . . The Allahabad High Court was to witness a cross-examination that would go down in the annals of Indian political history. Indira Gandhi herself was set to appear in court . . . And the outcome was destined to bring about a political revolution in the country,' remembers Prashant.

The Flashback

The 1971 general elections were an unusual event. President V.V. Giri had dissolved the Lok Sabha on 27 December 1970 on the advice of Indira Gandhi and called for elections that March. That was a year before the normal end of the five-year term, with elections under the regular scenario set for 1972.

Indira Gandhi had won that election with an overwhelming majority of more than 1.10 lakh votes. Her *Garibi Hatao* slogan had worked its magic!

Having lost miserably to Gandhi in Rae Bareli, socialist leader Raj Narain filed an election petition against her—one of the rarest and most sensational cases ever witnessed in the history of India. Prashant was lucky to have gotten the opportunity to witness the arguments. 'I would force my way through the crowded visitors' gallery, take extensive notes and try to decipher the outcome. Though the notes were meant to assist my father,

Shanti Bhushan, who was representing Raj Narain, in preparing the arguments for the case, little did I realize that in doing so, I had unknowingly sown the seeds of my own legal career,' Prashant said.

Justice Jagmohan Lal Sinha of the Allahabad High Court, who ultimately heard the case after Justice W. Broome retired, set aside Gandhi's election and disqualified her for a period of six years! It was a verdict that is still unparalleled in India's judicial and political history.

Even as Justice Sinha painstakingly read out the entire verdict, Prashant was not present in the court, but kept tracking the developments from Mumbai. However, it began to slowly dawn on him that his father had won the case! He stood transfixed, with a flood of emotions sweeping through him for the near-impossible victory his father had fought for and just won. Prashant knew at that very moment that he had witnessed one of the most significant moments in India's history!

The course of events that followed that fateful day gave rise to many questions. Was this how people become famous overnight? Can one important verdict in your favour make such a difference to your life? At least that seemed to be the case for his father! However, the path to achieving that verdict was every bit as laborious and painstaking as one can imagine, what with the scrupulous investigation and research work that went into solidifying a case. But it truly were the events of those heady days that gave birth to the lawyer in Prashant.

D-Day

It was around 9 a.m. when people started pouring into Court No. 24. This was the room where the cross-examination of Mrs Indira Gandhi was to take place. It was chosen because it was located right at the end of the court, and the restriction of the entry around it would not disturb the working of the other courtrooms.

There were several eminent politicians present in the court—Madhu Limaye, Shyam Nandan Prasad Mishra, Piloo Mody, Jyotirmoy Basu and Rabi Ray, who had all travelled from Delhi to witness the cross-examination. The proceedings were also witnessed by Rajiv and Sonia Gandhi.

At 9.58 a.m., when the judge arrived, everybody rose. Mrs Gandhi took a seat specially provided for her, unlike the normal practice where the witness stands in a witness box. This had been specially arranged by Justice Sinha in consultation with the defending counsel, Shanti Bhushan. Mrs Gandhi was seated on a raised platform to the right of the judge so that she was on par with the judge. And the proceedings began.

Prashant was merely nineteen at the time and clearly felt the trepidation himself and around the room. 'People will wonder what this history-making case was. What were the charges against Mrs Gandhi? What happened inside the courtrooms? What were the manoeuvrings that took place behind the scenes? I don't know if there was a writer hidden in me, but I felt a kind of moral obligation that the people of India and the future generations ought to know what transpired in this sensational case. A lot of things would have gone unreported and unnoticed had I not captured them in my first book: *The Case That Shook India*. It primarily deals with the queries mentioned above and goes on to track what happened on 25 June 1975. I must say that Justice Sinha raised the prestige of the judiciary,' Prashant said.

The case finally went to the Supreme Court and was heard at length. The ruling of the apex court too went against Indira Gandhi.

Early Life

Prashant was born into a family of lawyers in Allahabad on 15 October 1956. He was the eldest of four children of Shanti and Kumud Bhushan. His father was a lawyer-activist and a former Union law minister in the Morarji Desai government. His ancestors hailed from Sahanpur village in the Bijnor district of western Uttar Pradesh. His grandfather Vishwamitra too was a lawyer in Allahabad.

Prashant had spent his early childhood and formative years attending St Joseph's High School. He was fond of playing sports, though a typical day at school was more academics-oriented. Prashant used to play badminton, table tennis and tennis. 'Today, if time permits, I do some yoga. I like to remain fit, and for this I am quite regular with my yoga regime,' Prashant says.

He spent his childhood in Allahabad, known for its famous Kumbh Mela, the largest spiritual gathering in the world. In the 1960s, Allahabad was a vibrant, culturally active place, with music-loving people—enough to have an impact on the life of any teenager.

After passing out from St Joseph's, Prashant decided to pursue engineering at IIT Madras. However, after spending just a semester there, he decided to quit. There were no compelling circumstances, but there were two primary reasons for him to quit college in 1974. One, he realized that engineering wasn't really his cup of tea, and, two, he felt extremely homesick— mostly because of Shefali, his little sister. At that time, she was just two years old.

Prashant always believed that his father was quite supportive of all his decisions, but even he had advised him against dropping out of the prestigious IIT Madras. While Shanti Bhushan eventually came around to seeing his son's perspective, his mother was initially upset about Prashant's decision.

Undeterred, Prashant went on to enrol himself in a two-year BA programme to study philosophy, economics and political science in a college in his hometown of Allahabad. By this time he had become quite interested in the philosophy of science. He also had a good glimpse of the law because of Mrs Gandhi's election case. However, given the state of academic philosophy in India, he decided to formally enrol in an LLB programme. 'The law degree got delayed because of some student agitation and protest, and I had to wait till 1983 to appear for my final examination,' he added. Meanwhile, in 1979, he also began his doctorate in the philosophy of science at Princeton University, but eventually left in 1982 after completing his master's degree.

Prashant's adviser and professor at Princeton, Richard Carl Jeffrey, had even advised him to complete his doctorate, even if it meant working on the thesis in India. However, Prashant found it extremely difficult to complete the doctorate, given the amount of work it required, and realized that the master's degree in the philosophy of science was the most he could do academically. His father, Shanti Bhushan, had to undergo open-heart surgery around the time he was in Princeton, and it was perhaps another deciding factor for his leaving America. 'Sometimes, circumstances decide for you, as it did for me in this case,' Prashant said.

Meanwhile, he had witnessed a very turbulent decade, the years spanning 1970–80. India was now at the forefront of action and agitation. The decade was quite exciting and turbulent for India. Somewhere in the so-called 'developed' nations, scientists were busy carrying out space research programmes, but this part of the globe had witnessed a war, seen the creation of a neighbouring state, faced the Emergency being declared, and experienced social and political upheaval and large-scale imprisonment, not to mention impoverishment. In short, there was a lot to witness. Something was brewing during this decade, something that was to decide the course of Prashant's future career. Something that would give birth to a legal activist!

The Turning Point

The year 1975 proved to be a turning point. A lot has been chronicled about the history of India, let alone the history of the world during this year. It was also this very year that Prashant had his real tryst with the who's who of the legal world in Allahabad, including the likes of S.C. Khare.

The courtroom, the decorum, the code of conduct and, above all, the court proceedings could have inspired and motivated any budding young lawyer to excel and contribute to the legal system. Prashant was no exception. The early exposure and listening to arguments by eminent lawyers and the tough but challenging queries posed by the judges was enough to inspire him and light a fire in his belly.

Sitting in his Noida home, Prashant reminisces, 'Those five years when I was in Allahabad, after coming back from IIT, I read and thought about all kinds of philosophical issues, philosophical problems . . . I learnt to think about every issue, every problem on the basis of its principles.'

It was an important sort of intellectual training for him. The period of heavy pondering brought to the forefront the very essence of a lawyer. There are generally two kinds of lawyers according to Prashant. The first, who looks at legal problems from the angle of precedence, judgements and case laws; and the other, who looks at legal problems on the basis of first principles. 'I got this type of tutoring and mentoring from my father—to look at legal problems from first principles. After graduating in law, I got myself enrolled to practise law in Delhi. The "lawyer" in me was to a great extent nurtured by my father, but I have been a mama's boy too,' Prashant says, chuckling.

Prashant's mother, Kumud Bhushan, was simple at heart, and calm and composed. She loved to paint and dance. She organized family functions quite often and played the perfect host. However, it was yoga that would enliven her. She has had a profound influence in shaping Prashant's personality. 'The aesthetic sense and her love for the fine arts, including music, is something I have imbibed from her . . . even my social nature. She was the law at home,' Prashant reminisces fondly.

As a Lawyer

Prashant got enrolled with the Bar Council of Delhi in 1983 and started his legal career working with central government counsel Madan Lokur, who is a Supreme Court judge today. Back in those days, Justice Lokur had many cases in hand and Prashant worked with him on a voluntary basis. Working voluntarily was the usual practice for a fresh entrant who was not paid anything.

'It was a win-win situation for both of us. I was getting the necessary exposure and Madan was getting the required help. It is here that I also got the opportunity to handle cases independently,' says Prashant.

'My first independent case was before a central excise tribunal in 1983. And then, my first big case came through. How does limestone act as an aquifer? It was this scientific issue that brought environmental activist Vandana Shiva to offer the Doon Valley case to me,' he said. Limestone-mining operations in the Doon Valley had become widespread during that time. Unabated and illegal mining had caused widespread land degradation, and this, in turn, had drastically affected the fragile ecosystem. Tree coverage and lush green forests had started disappearing.

Blasting and mining the hills had affected and shaken the foundations of the earth. Rocks and scree (a collection of accumulated broken rock fragments) rolled down and killed and injured the cattle, also damaging the cultivable land. With the felling of the forest, the rain became less frequent, and with the limestone dug out, the aquifers ceased to exist. The high deposits of scree and stones interrupted the flow of water, and Dehradun's water supply—even for drinking—was substantially reduced. This unscientific and uncontrolled limestone-quarrying operation had endangered the ecological balance.

Prashant says, remembering the case, 'I felt the gravity of the situation and filed a writ petition on Vandana's request. She inspired me. She was the first person who encouraged me to file a PIL in 1983—the year I began my practice in earnest—against limestone mining in the Doon Valley. My scientific knowledge came in handy.'

This case became the starting point of Prashant's long but successful journey as a legal activist. 'Civil rights violations during the Emergency dragged me into civil liberty issues and, now, I had this environmental cause to fight for. It was at this point in my life that I decided to join PUCL [People's Union of Civil Liberties], and gradually I got involved in PILs,' Prashant points out.

It was in 1990 that, with the help of some eminent lawyers, ex-judges and his father, Prashant was successful in establishing the Committee on Judicial Accountability (CJA) primarily to fight corruption in the judiciary, and bring about some accountability without compromising on its independence. The underpinning was to foster transparency and accountability.

His Forte: PILs

'PILs were to become my forte. The 2G spectrum scam, Coalgate, the fracas over the Radia tapes, coal and iron-ore mining scams—these had all alerted the government and put the corporate world in trouble. I took the onus of explaining to the court how the former telecom minister A. Raja, the prime accused in the 2G spectrum scam, had allegedly committed serious irregularities in the grant of licences and had caused a huge loss to the exchequer to the tune of Rs 1.76 lakh crore, as per the national auditor's figures. I think it was due to my initiative that the apex court cancelled all 122 licences on 2 February 2012 and ordered a re-auction,' Prashant says with some degree of pride about the impact his work has had on the country's economy.

The list is endless. Prashant was also instrumental in initiating and handling the PIL for the coal block allocations. Along with advocate M.L. Sharma, he made the Supreme Court declare as arbitrary and illegal, more than 204 government allocations of coal blocks to steel, cement and power companies since 1993. The national auditor, the Comptroller and Auditor General of India, in 2012 had claimed that this allocation, popularly dubbed 'Coalgate', had cost losses worth Rs 1.86 lakh crore to the state exchequer. 'I initiated the PIL to seek the cancellation of coal block allocations on the ground that rules were flouted to favour certain companies,' Prashant points out.

Even the country's top court removed the then CBI director, Ranjit Sinha, barely twelve days before his retirement, from the 2G spectrum case, after Prashant informed the apex court that he had tried to influence the probe and even helped some of the accused. The Supreme Court found that the allegations made by the Centre for Public Interest Litigation (CPIL), an NGO that Prashant represented, had some credibility. 'I requested Prime Minister Narendra Modi to remove the CBI chief for his interference in the high-profile 2G case as well as in the Coalgate scam. The court also recalled its earlier order that had directed CPIL to disclose the name of the whistle-blower who had provided documents (entry register at Sinha's home and other file notes) to me. The documents prove that Sinha was holding private meetings at his official residence with those facing CBI probes in the 2G spectrum and Coalgate scams. Sinha was overseeing the probe in both the cases that are being monitored by the Supreme Court,' Prashant says.

It was on the basis of his PIL that the Supreme Court in 2011 set aside P.J. Thomas's appointment as head of the anti-corruption body, the Central Vigilance Commission, and also laid down stringent guidelines for such appointments. The court quashed a September 2010 central government recommendation for the appointment of Thomas as Central Vigilance Commissioner as 'illegal' since the high-powered panel had failed to consider the pending charge-sheet in the palmolein-import scam against him.

In 2013, the apex court imposed a ban on iron-ore mining in Goa and allowed the resumption of operations with a cap of 20 million tonnes a year, after only eighteen months of the ban. Environmental degradation and illegal mining has taken a toll on mines and mineral-rich states. The Supreme Court allowed the reopening of various categories of mines in Karnataka after a year-long ban, and only after laying down the road map for how mining licences were to be given to companies. Given the huge negative impact these mining activities were having on the surrounding environment, Prashant decided to file a PIL seeking the cancellation of mining licences in areas where rampant illegal mining was observed in the state.

In an another PIL against the government, Prashant alleged that the Mukesh Ambani–run Reliance Jio Infocomm Ltd had been given an undue benefit of more than Rs 20,000 crore by allowing it to offer voice services on its 4G spectrum by converting its Internet service provider (ISP) licence into a unified access services licence. Prashant had objected to this move and had questioned why the government had allowed the company voice-telephony on a payment of a meagre Rs 1658 crore, a price determined way back in 2001. The case is pending before the Supreme Court.

Prashant admits that he may have crossed one line too many with the various scathing PILs he has been pursuing. 'My voicing of problems in the judiciary, and talking about judicial corruption also brought me in conflict with the judiciary,' he said. In an interview to a magazine in 2009, he took on the Supreme Court judges. 'I feel that at least half of the sixteen former Chief Justices in the Supreme Court were corrupt. I was promptly served a contempt notice for this kind of a comment,' Prashant rues.

One of the country's leading lawyers Harish Salve filed a contempt case in 2010 against Prashant for the accusations he had made against the judges, questioning their integrity. The legal activist was given an opportunity to apologize to the judges hearing the matter. While Prashant did not tender an apology, he did file an explanation with the apex court as to why he thought the integrity of some of the judges was not of the highest levels. The matter has now been put in cold storage.

Pursuant to this contempt case in 2010, another unusual thing happened in 2011. 'I was attacked by the members of the Bhagat Singh Kranti Sena inside the Supreme Court premises. This was in reaction to my stand on the Kashmir issue. I was dragged out of my chair and repeatedly kicked and punched, that too in front of a TV crew and journalists,' Prashant relates. It was undoubtedly a horrific incident.

'I think my stand on Kashmir has been misinterpreted. It has been misinterpreted, misunderstood and twisted. The context of a referendum has been misconstrued. A referendum is referred to decide whether or not the army should be deployed to deal with internal threats in Kashmir,' says Prashant. 'The army or paramilitary forces have been provided impunity by the Armed Forces (Jammu and Kashmir) Special Powers Act, 1990, which means that even if they commit murder or rape in the state, they are hardly ever charged for it, thus encouraging all kinds of human rights violations. As a human rights activist, my concern was to raise this issue. There is no good reason to have these armed forces provide impunity, or to even force so many army personnel on Kashmiris for their own internal security. They don't want this kind of security for themselves—why should it be forced upon them? It's a different matter to have security at the borders—that the government can certainly deploy. But most of the army personnel are not for border security, they are used for internal security . . . they are posted deep inside Kashmir, all over Kashmir,' says Prashant.

Unforgettable 1984

In 1984, Prashant married Deepa, a Sikh girl who happened to be a practising lawyer and was also his father's junior associate. Shanti Bhushan was rather fond of the girl, as was Prashant's grandmother. Deepa practised in the courts for about three years following the marriage, but decided to quit when their first son, Manav, was born.

In 1984, Indira Gandhi was assassinated. The ensuing riots that tore the nation apart pursuant to her death bore an indelible mark on Prashant's psyche, becoming the major reason for him getting involved with numerous civil liberties organizations. Six years later, in 1990, he published his second book, *Bofors: The Selling of a Nation,* an investigation into the Bofors scam that had rocked the nation and had embroiled the then prime minister, Rajiv Gandhi, along with several other eminent personalities in it. It also became the major reason for Rajiv Gandhi losing the elections.

The Bofors scam was a defence scam, and was considered a hallmark of corruption in Indian politics. Bofors became a buzzword in the Indian political arena, and amidst this backdrop rose the eminent politician V.P. Singh. It was former prime minister V.P. Singh who has been credited with taking the initiative to send letters rogatory to Switzerland. Later, when Narisimha Rao took charge as the prime minister, the then foreign minister Madhavsinh Solanki played a proactive role to mitigate the scam effect. In his attempt to halt the investigation, he'd sent a note to the concerned Swiss authority. Unfortunately, this note was leaked, and with it ended the political career of Solanki.

It's been more than twenty-five years, but the ghost of Bofors still re-emerges at times.

The Bhopal Gas Tragedy: A Haunting Spectre

On the night of 2–3 December 1984, a poisonous gas leaked from the premises of the Union Carbide fertilizer unit in Bhopal, killing and disabling thousands of the city's citizens. The tragedy that till today is marked as one of the world's worst industrial accidents rattled the nation. Prashant was shaken up, almost furious with the way the government of the day had reacted to the mammoth tragedy. 'I was quite upset with the outcome of the settlement of the Bhopal gas tragedy case, and I had approached Arun Shourie, the then editor of the *Indian Express*, and who later became the disinvestment, communication and IT minister, to highlight the injustice done to the victims,' Prashant says. 'Why don't you write about it?' Shourie had suggested to Prashant.

'"Judgement of the Court or Capitulation by the Government", the article written by me on 17 February 1989 was carried on the front pages of all *Indian Express* editions,' Prashant reminisces. He spoke fearlessly through his writings within two days of the Supreme Court judgement delivered on

14 February 1989. Much later, it was Shourie who had suggested to Prashant that he write a book on the Rs 64 crore-Bofors scam. That's how the idea of writing his book, *Bofors: The Selling of a Nation*, materialized.

As the world prepared to welcome the new millennium, Prashant remained occupied with his share of contributions to the legal fraternity. Prashant turned forty in 1996 and, by this time, he had made a name for himself. He was fortunate enough to handle a wide spectrum of legal matters—environmental issues, civil liberty matters, civil rights and human rights issues, social justice, corruption matters and all kinds of public interest issues. 'People and budding young lawyers now shower extraordinary attention on me and often turn up and request a tête-à-tête,' Prashant says. It was during one of those usual lunch hours when a young man turned up and greeted him.

Chamber 301

Simplicity, sincerity and accessibility are some of the unique traits that Prashant has imbibed from his mother. He is easily accessible and approachable, and if one is fortunate, they can walk into his Supreme Court New Lawyers Chamber No. 301 for a conversation.

'Namaste, sir, how are you?' said the young man.

'Namaste,' Prashant greeted him.

For a moment, Prashant had mistaken him for a probable client. But the very next moment the man said something that took Prashant by surprise. 'Sir, you've have been my role model all through.' With gleaming eyes he continued, *'Main aap ke jaisa banna chahta hoon.'* ['I want to be like you'.]

'Compliments are rare in life, especially those coming from the heart. This, I felt, was one such case, and I wanted to help this young man out in whatever manner I could,' says Prashant, remembering the day. 'What is so special about me?' Prashant had asked the man. 'I like the way you connect with the common man, the common cause . . . your concern for the environment and your fight against corruption,' the young man had said, almost star-struck. But then he asked Prashant something that made the astute legal activist reflect deep within him. The young man asked, 'Sir, you must have a role model too? Are you inspired by your father?'

On his way back home to Noida, these questions reverberated with Prashant. 'It was difficult to have any one person be my role model. I think I admire some qualities of my father, not all. I admire some qualities of Delhi chief minister Arvind Kejriwal. He is very bold, fearless, totally committed, extremely bright, sharp, and politically astute—but he has his weaknesses too,' Prashant says, pointing out the people from varied walks of life from whom he's learnt immeasurably.

There have been people who have had an impact on Prashant in the formative years of his legal profession. Prominent among them was the late Hardev Singh, the convener of the CJA. He was a man of great principles. 'The list could be endless, but I think I have profound admiration for Justice P.N. Bhagwati's judicial acumen, the late Justice Krishna Iyer's judicial acumen and boundless compassion, and Justice M.N. Venkatachaliah's integrity and judicial acumen,' Prashant says. He also holds Justice G.S. Singhvi, the author of the 2G spectrum judgement, in high esteem for his hard-working nature and for his absolute integrity and willingness to come down hard against corruption.

A senior journalist reporting at the Supreme Court once told Prashant, 'You have a visionary attitude . . . I am sure you have cultivated it and not imbibed it from someone.' In response to this, he says, 'I have been involved in so many different issues, both as a lawyer as well as an activist. Therefore, I think I have been able to look at the country and the world from a vantage point where I can see the connections between various issues,' Prashant says, pointing out how he, as an individual, has evolved over the years.

Prashant has cultivated the ability to look at what's happening around and, over a period of time, it has become relatively easier for him to understand the connections between all the instruments of power—how the whole ruling establishment, the judiciary functions and various other institutions function.

K.K. Venugopal, a senior Supreme Court lawyer says, 'According to me, he has done more for the country than any other lawyer. He has brought to the notice of the court the black, or negative, side of governance and ensured that the court intervenes and corrects the area of criminal law and corruption. And all this was made possible because of his association with CPIL and Common Cause, the two NGOs.'

'Prashant has done a tremendous amount of work. He is too intense—he cannot sit back and think objectively. He cannot think of the matter from the viewpoint of the opposite side. Therefore, if he finds that something is being said against him, he straightaway flares up, and has often been seen to resort to shouting,' says another senior lawyer who is pitched against him in the high-profile 2G spectrum scam. Another lawyer adds, 'He starts his arguments at a very high pitch and after some time is unable to sustain that pitch. But then I would say that he has done more good than any of the other lawyers.'

Raian Karanjawala, the managing director of Karanjawala & Co., says, 'Prashant has his own impact. He is in the area of public law and public space, and he has made his own contributions, and certainly, when he speaks in the courts on the matter on public issues, people do take him with a very high level of seriousness.

They see in him a certain sincerity. They see a lot of the sacrifices he has made. The judges also take him seriously.'

A Perfect Lawyer

Given the current climate of corruption, it is very important to hold up a certain level of integrity, and that is also why this question often troubles Prashant, compelling him to search and reflect deeper—what makes a perfect lawyer? His answer to this question is what makes Prashant the individual he is today. He says, 'I feel lawyers must have a sense of justice; a lawyer is not meant to be a mercenary the way that unfortunately most of our 'big lawyers' have become. They are guns for hire, so to say, they are willing to go and kill anybody . . . I mean, protect any crooked person in order to make money.'

He says money has become the sole objective of this profession in today's culture. It's sad and quite unfortunate. A lawyer is supposed to be a civilized warrior for justice, he must have some sense to differentiate between the just and the unjust. Today, there are many lawyers who are being paid only to get adjournments, who come to the court and make big money only from adjournments. They are called 'adjournment lawyers'. On the other hand, there are lawyers who are very active now because of the anti-corruption movement and the awareness that has been created. They can best be described as 'judicial activists'.

The other question that has of late preoccupied Prashant more than he would admit is: What should the role of the judiciary be? He explains it rather adeptly. 'The role of the judiciary is to act as a watchdog of the executive and the legislature. Unfortunately, the judiciary rarely performs this kind of job.'

On the issue of judicial appointments, Prashant feels that appointing judges needs to be completely independent of anything else, and he is also not so open to the idea of having a code of procedure for judges. This code is a mere ideology. Prashant has been quite upfront about the corruption in the judiciary and the need for transparency in judicial appointments.

His Approach

Prashant has always had his own parameters and criteria to choose cases, and to a great extent, it is his conscience and experience that have helped him decide the damage factor that a case can cause to public interest. 'I normally see how serious the injustice is or how important the public interest is with regard to the case that has been brought to me. The issue which needs to be taken up is thoroughly researched. If I know somebody who understands that issue well, then I usually ask him or her to do the research and to get back to me,' Prashant says, explaining the way he chooses cases to fight.

He only takes up a case, be it a private case or a PIL, if he feels that the cause is just. 'I do not take up cases like the many mercenary lawyers in this country do, who take up cases on behalf of people whom they know. Their cause is totally unjust, and the client is usually totally crooked or corrupt. People are often curious to know what I charge my clients. The PILs I do are more activism, in which one has to reconcile oneself with little income and next to no potential to earn much money. That's because in public-interest cases, one is not expected to charge any money. I don't charge any fee in public-interest cases,' says Prashant.

Fortunately, financial assistance has not been a problem for Prashant. His father being a successful commercial lawyer is of much help. 'For me, money is not a constraint, but I understand that it can be one for many people who do not come from such a privileged background,' he says.

Of course, not too many of these important public-interest cases meet with success; only a small percentage of them are eventually successful. Most of them keep languishing for a long time; only a small percentage reach any successful conclusion. So in that sense it can also be frustrating. 'One has to get used to the fact that in the kind of judicial system we have today, this is how things will be. One has to feel satisfied with those few successful cases if you can learn to derive satisfaction from them,' he points out.

According to Pranav Sachdeva, a young junior lawyer who is a part of almost every case being handled by Prashant, 'Mr Bhushan's complete dedication to the public cause, coupled with total selflessness, is an example for all patriotic citizens. For the last six years, I have seen the passion he brings to public-interest matters—for which he refuses to charge any money. He is also a soft-spoken gentleman at all times, except in the courtroom, where he seems to be on fire.'

Prashant says that he has always dreamt of setting up a public-interest organization to further the prospect of creating awareness about public litigation and public policies. The Sambhaavnaa Institute for Public Policy and Politics in Palampur, Himachal Pradesh, does exactly this kind of work. 'The institute is largely financed by my father. It's an institute which runs three kinds of programmes for people who want to become activists and work on public policies and politics. The course offers modules of education, training and motivation to equip these young minds with a better understanding of policies, strategies, and how to take these policies forward,' Prashant says. Then there are programmes meant to educate and inspire students to think about the model of development that India has embarked upon, the effect of the model on the various sections of society, as well as the various alternatives to this model. The whole idea is to inspire and sensitize students to these developing issues.

'I feel that these skills are important because, normally, people in the country just want to find some job without really trying to understand how this particular job is helping the country, how it is affecting other people, or how it is serving or harming public interest. The idea is that students should become more aware and sensitive to these issues,' Prashant points out.

Hall of Legal Fame

The reasons for Prashant Bhushan to figure in the Hall of Legal Fame are many, but the focus area would be his judicial and social activism. His viewpoint pertaining to corruption in the judiciary and judicial accountability is a reflection on judicial governance. He is actively engaged in PILs, and is quite a central figure in cases that relate to human rights, environmental protection and matters dealing with the accountability of public servants.

Many people may not know this, but Prashant has the unique distinction of drafting each and every impeachment motion against any judge that has ever been presented. He is often considered a modern hero, the people's advocate who argues for the common man and champions the cause of whistle-blowers and rickshaw pullers. He was also one of the key players in the Lokpal movement, where he has sought a platform to fight corruption. To counter prevailing corrupt practices, the Aam Aadmi Party, which came to power in Delhi, was seen as his ideal platform.

His Daily Life

A strict disciplinarian, Prashant follows a daily routine. He is regular with his yoga, and the evenings are usually spent in meetings—

generally political, and occasionally some media interaction. He retires to bed by 11 p.m. The only time he doesn't adhere to this schedule is when he is travelling. Prashant travels to his hometown, Allahabad, about once a year. Once in every three years or so, he makes it a point to visit the Jindal Naturecure Institute, Bangalore, with his wife, as he has deep faith in naturopathy.

Prashant is fond of and enjoys all kinds of music; he has a fascination for music concerts. He likes to listen to old Hindi-film songs, but is particularly fond of Indian classical music, specifically Pandit Jasraj and Pandit Bhimsen Joshi. He also listens to ghazals by Jagjit Singh. One can often find him tuning into bhajans while doing yoga.

Prashant has a penchant for current affairs and economics, and also likes reading books, particularly the works of Joseph Stiglitz and Bertrand Russell. He also likes reading on nutrition, health and healing.

'Shallow men believe in luck. Strong men believe in cause and effect'—these words by Ralph Waldo Emerson make one think of Prashant Bhushan.

THE CASE

Centre for Public Interest Litigation v. Union of India
with
Dr Subramanian Swamy v. Union of India
Judgement delivered by bench comprising Justices G.S. Singhvi and Asok Kumar Ganguly on 2 February 2012

Case Details
Holding allocation of second-generation (2G) spectrum by the Congress–led UPA government 'illegal' and arbitrary

exercise of power, the Supreme Court cancelled all 122 telecom licences allotted on or after 10 January 2008 to eleven companies during the tenure of former telecom minister, A. Raja.

Allowing writ petitions filed by CPIL and others, and Janata Party president, Subramanian Swamy, seeking the cancellation of the licences, the court further ruled that spectrum being a scarce natural resource is vested with the government as a matter of trust in the name of the people of India, and the state is duty-bound to protect the national interest of the country and not private interests.

The apex court observed there was a fundamental flaw in the first-come, first-served principle, inasmuch as it 'involves an element of pure chance or accident'. And in the matters involving the award of contracts or grant of licence or permission to use public property, the invocation of the first-come, first-served principle had inherently dangerous implications.

While the original plan for awarding spectrum licences was to follow a first-come, first-served policy to applicants, Raja allegedly manipulated the rules so that the policy would kick in—not on the basis of who applied first, but who complied with the terms and conditions first.

Raja, in conspiracy with the other co-accused, had advanced the cut-off date from 1 October 2007 to 25 September 2007, to favour Unitech Wireless (Tamil Nadu) Limited and Swan Telecom, promoted by co-accused Shahid Usman Balwa. Even on 10 January 2008, companies were given just a few hours to provide their letters of intent and cheques. Those allegedly tipped off by Raja were ready with their cheques and other documents.

The Supreme Court had held: 'The licences granted to the private respondents—Etisalat DB Telecom (Swan Telecom), Unitech Wireless, Loop Telecom, Videocon Telecommunications, S-Tel Ltd, Allianz Infratech, Idea Cellular and Aditya Birla Telecom (Space Communications), Tata Teleservices, Sistema Shyam Tele Services (Shyam Telelink), Dishnet Wireless and Vodafone Essar South—on or after 10 January 2008, pursuant to two press releases issued on that date, and the subsequent allocation of spectrum to the licencees are declared illegal and are quashed.' The court further mandated that affected licence holders could operate for four months, during which regulators would come up with new market rules.

The cancelled licences included twenty-one of Videocon Telecommunications, twenty-two of Unitech Wireless Ltd (Uninor), nine of Idea Cellular, twenty-one of Loop Telecom, six of S-Tel Ltd, twenty-one of Sistema Shyam Tele Services (Shyam Telelink), three of Tata Teleservices, thirteen of Etisalat DB Telecom (Swan Telecom) and two of Allianz Infratech.

The proceedings in the case conducted by the special CBI court, set up exclusively to deal with the 2G spectrum case, are also being monitored by the Supreme Court.

Apart from Raja, DMK leader and Rajya Sabha MP M. Kanimozhi, who is also the daughter of former Tamil Nadu chief minister M. Karunanidhi, former telecom secretary Siddharth Behura, Raja's erstwhile private secretary R.K. Chandolia, Swan Telecom promoters, Shahid Usman Balwa and Vinod Goenka, Unitech Ltd MD Sanjay Chandra, three top executives of Reliance Anil Dhirubhai Ambani

Group, Gautam Doshi, Surendra Pipara and Hari Nair, are all facing trial in the case. The directors of Kusegaon Fruits and Vegetables Pvt. Ltd, Asif Balwa and Rajiv Agarwal, Kalaignar TV director Sharad Kumar, and Bollywood producer Karim Morani are also accused in the case.

Three telecom firms—Swan Telecom Pvt. Ltd, Reliance Telecom Ltd and Unitech Wireless (Tamil Nadu) Ltd—have also been arrayed as the accused in the first two CBI charge-sheets filed on 2 and 25 April 2011 respectively.

The CBI on 12 December 2011 filed its charge sheet against Essar Group promoters, Ravi Ruia and Anshuman Ruia, and Loop Telecom promoters, I.P. Khaitan and Kiran Khaitan, for their alleged role in the criminal case linked to the 2G scam. Essar Group director (strategy and planning), Vikash Saraf, and three telecom firms, Loop Telecom Pvt. Ltd, Loop Mobile India Ltd and Essar Tele Holdings Ltd, were also arrayed as accused in the charge sheet for allegedly cheating the Department of Telecom by using Loop Telecom as a 'front' to secure 2G licences in 2008.

CBI judge O.P. Saini has framed charges against them under various provisions of the Indian Penal Code and the Prevention of Corruption Act, dealing with offences of criminal conspiracy, cheating, forgery, faking documents, abusing one's official position, criminal misconduct by a public servant and taking bribes. The offences entail punishment ranging from six months in jail to life imprisonment.

In the second case in the 2G spectrum allocation scam, special judge O.P. Saini has so far framed charges and put on trial nineteen of the accused—ten individuals and nine companies—in 'parking' of illegal gratification of Rs 200 crore in Kalaignar TV, under money-laundering laws. The individuals include Raja, Kanimozhi, Shahid Usman Balwa and Vinod Goenka. If convicted, the accused will face a maximum sentence of up to seven years. At present, all the accused are out on bail.

Even the Supreme Court had quashed the CBI court's order summoning Bharti Group chairman, Sunil Mittal, and Essar's vice chairman, Ravi Ruia, as accused in the excess spectrum allotment case of 2002 when the NDA government was in power.

While Mittal and Ruia's names were not in the CBI charge-sheet as the accused, Saini had, in March 2013, summoned them, stating that there was enough material to proceed against them. Besides the three, the court had also summoned as the accused former telecom secretary Shyamal Ghosh, and three telecom firms: Bharti Cellular, Hutchison Max Telecom (now known as Vodafone India) and Sterling Cellular (now known as Vodafone Mobile Service).

The CBI charge-sheet had only named the companies as accused but not any of its executives.

Impact

The 2G spectrum scam was a major telecommunications scam in which politicians and bureaucrats had colluded to give away a scarce natural resource to ineligible companies at throwaway prices. The ruling came as an embarrassment for the UPA government, led by the then prime minister Manmohan Singh, which oversaw the sale of the licences at below-market prices.

While the Comptroller and Auditor General of India had pegged the loss to the exchequer at Rs 1.76 lakh crore, the then telecom minister Kapil Sibal had claimed that 'zero loss' was caused by the distribution of 2G licences on a first-come, first-served basis.

In 2011, *Time* magazine listed the scam at number two on their list of the top ten abuses of power—just behind the Watergate scandal.

While the anti-corruption brigade had hailed the judgement, telecos, investors, banks and experts fumed about the prospect of billions going down the drain. They felt the judgement would impact future investments in the country, dent investor confidence and strengthen the perception that government policies can be easily overturned by the courts. 'It is a historic judgement. It is trying to break a corrupt nexus between business and politics,' said political analyst Paranjoy Guha Thakurta, one of petitioners in the case.

Foreign investors—Norway's Telenor and Russia's Sistema Shyam—claimed they had only followed government policies in place at the time. Both operators had entered into joint ventures with the Indian companies that were awarded licences by Raja.

Banks had varied exposure to the telecom companies involved in the case. The country's largest lender, the State Bank of India, said the bank had a fund-based exposure of Rs 1100 crore in telecom companies affected by the apex court's order.

Though the cancellation had resulted in reviving investor uncertainty of doing business in Asia's third-biggest economy for a short while, the Supreme Court's reiteration to allocate scarce natural resources only at market-determined prices, or through auctions, is a step closer to transparency and accountability.

Winning Strokes
Questioning the grant of unified access services licences to private companies, Prashant Bhushan had contended that the spectrum, which is a national asset, cannot be distributed by adopting the principle of first-come, first-served, and that too without any advertisement and without holding an auction.

Raja's decision to advance the cut-off date from 1 October 2007 to 25 September 2007, which eliminated a large number of telecos, was violative of Article 14 of the Constitution, and the entire exercise undertaken with reference to this cut-off date had resulted in discrimination vis-à-vis other eligible applicants as well, according to Prashant.

He pointed out that although the prime minister had suggested that a fair and transparent method be adopted for the grant of unified access services licences through the process of auction, the Minister of Communications and Information Technology casually and arbitrarily brushed aside the suggestion and granted licences to ineligible companies for extraneous reasons.

According to Bhushan, when it comes to the alienation of scarce natural resources like spectrum, etc., the state must always adopt the method of auction by giving wide publicity, so that all eligible persons may participate in the process. Any other methodology for disposal of public property and natural resources/national assets is likely to be misused by unscrupulous people who are only interested in garnering maximum financial benefit and have no respect for constitutional ethos and values.

He further said that a failure to comply with the roll-out conditions was a serious matter since the scarce spectrum and telecom licences were given for the benefit of the consumers. If no service was started by the operators in spite of the fact that they got the licences and spectrum at throwaway prices, then their licences should have been immediately suspended or cancelled.

Prashant was opposed by a battery of senior lawyers— the late Attorney General of India G.E. Vahanvati, and senior lawyers including Harish Salve, Aryama Sundaram, Vikas Singh, C.S. Vaidyanathan, Abhishek Manu Singhvi and Rakesh Dwivedi, among others.

VII

JUSTICE ROHINTON F. NARIMAN: THE GOLD STANDARD

Born on 13 August 1956 in Mumbai

What is wisdom without courage?
What is intelligence without vision?
What are good thoughts and good words
without good deeds?
And what is wealth without generosity?
—Unknown

ROHINTON NARIMAN[*] began his journey to adulthood with an unlikely scenario. He was going to do one of the most challenging things in his life, something he had been preparing for a month. Few can realize the magnitude of a task unless they have been through it themselves.

'This is going to be a Herculean task,' said a community member.

'How old are you, my child?' asked a member in the congregation.

'Twelve,' he replied.

'What a darling boy. God bless you, my son,' replied the elderly gentleman.

Young Rohinton did not understand what 'Herculean' meant. He had no idea of the task expected of him. He was destined to do this daunting task and, to the amazement of many, he did it. He had been expected to memorize something like the entire Rig Veda. 'To cut a long story short, it was my initiation into spirituality. I was ordained as a priest at the very young age of twelve from the Bandra Agiary,' he says.

---

[*] The author spoke to Rohinton Nariman when he was practising as a lawyer. The chapter has thus been considerably streamlined for relevancy.

However, Rohinton never chose to be one, nor was the same imposed on him. Bapsi Nariman, his mother, was instrumental in his becoming a priest. She encouraged and inspired him. She wanted him to continue the tradition. He belonged to a 'priestly' family (from his father's side), but neither his father nor grandfather had undergone the rigorous rituals of priesthood. So to keep his mother's heart, Rohinton willingly opted for the rigorous training. It was challenging to say the least.

It took Rohinton about a month's time. He had to stay inside the *agyari*—the fire temple—for twenty-eight days at a stretch, only among priests, pray five times a day and face restrictions on touching any person. He was not allowed to meet his family during that period of intense training. His companions during that period were a family of very kind-hearted priests, who also had a great sense of fun, so although it was difficult, Rohinton remembers that period of his life with great fondness.

Being an obedient child, he observed the required discipline and followed all the stringent rules. 'I was made to cram Zoroastrian scriptures in my younger days at the religious seminaries during my initiation into priesthood. Later, this type of training helped me in my professional career. It helped me remember and cite things verbatim,' Rohinton says.

Fast forward several years later to London. 'Amazing!' exclaimed a passer-by, who happened to witness an interesting incident that took place on a bright afternoon.

Some eight years ago, Rohinton was holidaying in London with his wife, Sanaya. On one of their sightseeing excursions, they had visited the famous Westminster Abbey. Now, there was a board showing the line-up of the kings and queens of England. Rohinton, being interested in the genealogy of royal families, stood up, scrutinizing the list. There was something amiss and he knew it.

Rohinton stood behind the board and told his wife to cross-check as he rattled off the names.

'That one is incorrect,' said Sanaya.

'Impossible,' replied Rohinton.

'Here, you can check the board yourself,' she said.

He was taken aback. 'It can't be. The board is wrong,' he said.

The Narimans decided to meet the curator to cross-check if his discovery of a factual error on the board was indeed correct. It so turns out that Rohinton was right—a testament to his brilliant memory and intelligence. 'Thank you for bringing to our notice the error on our board,' was the short but grateful note that Rohinton received from the curator in London a few days following the incident.

Rohinton Fali Nariman was appointed a judge of the Supreme Court of India on 7 July 2014, becoming only the fifth lawyer to be elevated to the position of a judge of the apex court after almost fifteen years. 'It's a lifetime achievement,' says Sanaya proudly.

The law and Rohinton—the two go together. And the journey has been quite rewarding, a journey without any fear or favour.

The Background

Priesthood did not mean his school days were over. He attended the Cathedral and John Connon School in Mumbai, and is still in touch with his former classmates and favourite teachers.

But the school didn't really help him to grow. It was a school with a large number of students from rich families. 'I vividly remember those children who had 100 rupees and would flash it around, as against my pocket money of 25 paisa a week. The best I could do with my pocket money in those days was to buy either lemon drops or one Coke,' he says.

His childhood days were not so happy. His teachers were very strict, and some would often beat him. And then there those children who were pretty rough with him as well; being a mild-mannered child he would often get bullied. 'I was brought up in a strict environment, and had a middle-class kind of upbringing. And that I believe was the best thing that could happen to me,' Rohinton says.

However, Rohinton grew up to be a very aggressive person. This transformation was mainly because he had to fight his way up to his present position. 'Growing up was indeed challenging. I owe a lot to my mother and my grandparents for all their input and support when I was growing up in the vibrant city of Mumbai,' he says.

The Gateway of India is one such spot in Mumbai where you find a cosmopolitan mix of culture and people from all parts of India and the world and from all walks of life. Whoever visits the business capital of India would make it to this historical monument built during the British Raj. It's a delightful experience to view the vast expanse of the Arabian Sea stretching away from the Gateway of India. Just opposite to it stands the majestic Taj Mahal Palace hotel. Rohinton's maternal grandfather was a building contractor who had followed his father's footsteps. He had worked with British architects to build magnificent structures as well as the old customs house and the Bombay High Court. 'I grew up watching both the great Gateway of India and the Taj and, deep down, my closeness to this magnificence would often make me smile,' he says.

Rohinton's Journey to Becoming a Lawyer

Rohinton has had a long walk and a measured stride. People often say that if you want to walk fast, walk alone, and if you want to walk far, walk with someone. For Rohinton, his beliefs and conscience have been his constant companions.

What brought him so far is a story in itself. His journey began with a baffling question: If not a priest, then what would he like to be? 'I don't know what I was waiting for. Maybe something would happen by design or chance. Was I interested in music? I was not sure.' Finally, Rohinton decided to take up the law, the profession of his famous father, who cast a deep shadow that Rohinton was determined to step out of, and emerge into his own.

Fali S. Nariman, Rohinton's father, is an eminent jurist and one of the most prominent lawyers in India today. He began his career in the Bombay High Court and has since been active in the legal profession. Over the years, he has held several prestigious posts at both the national and international levels. He was appointed the Additional Solicitor General of India in 1972, and became a member of Parliament (Rajya Sabha) in November 1999. He is also a recipient of the Padma Bhushan (in 1991) and the Padma Vibhushan (in 2007).

Chance, coincidence and destiny are not merely abstractions but the chief architects of life. It is destined that one must play one's own little instrument in the orchestra of life. When, where and how—these are questions that are inevitably answered in the passage of life.

'In my case, it happened when I was in class nine. I ended up taking commerce by default. Why I took it up, I don't know. I think I was inspired by my teachers. I had a fascination for the subject and so completed my high school education in commerce. Later, I graduated in commerce from SRCC [the Shri Ram College of Commerce], Delhi. By this time, my father had become a law officer and was posted in Delhi. He helped me join a chartered accountancy firm. I had a month-long stint there,' says Rohinton.

Talent and intelligence are God-given, and Rohinton had them in abundance. Fali Nariman recalls an incident from Rohinton's college days. 'When he [Rohinton] was in college, he won a prize in some debating competition, and was awarded a certain sum of money and a medal. But he turned it down and gave it to the man who stood second because he felt that this man had a genuine need. He made a sacrifice, but never boasted about it ever again.' He continues, 'I feel proud of my son. He is generous, and is a genuinely good-hearted person.'

'Chartered accountancy was not for me, not at all,' says Rohinton. Left with very few options after obtaining his BCom (Hons) degree, he felt that law would be his best bet. He completed his LLB from the Faculty of Law, University of Delhi. He was amongst the toppers. He joined the Delhi Bar as an advocate in 1974. He then attended the prestigious Harvard Law School. 'It was at Harvard that I submitted my thesis: "Affirmative Action: A Comparison between Indian and US Constitutional Law".' It is the expertise he obtained here that turned out to be the starting point of a long and illustrious career for Rohinton, not only as a constitutional lawyer but as a part of the Supreme Court Constitutional Bench immediately after being appointed as a judge. Incidentally, Rohinton's eldest daughter, Nina, also attended Harvard, obtaining her LLM degree in 2011.

Rohinton was fortunate enough to spend a year with eminent jurist Nani Palkhivala before leaving for Harvard. He had the opportunity to assist him in the famous *Minerva Mills* case (1980) being heard at the Supreme Court. The important five-judge Constitutional Bench headed by the then Chief Justice of India Y.V. Chandrachud, in the landmark case unanimously extended the basic structure doctrine and held that Parliament cannot take away the fundamental rights of individuals, including the right to liberty and equality. The ruling struck down Sections 4 and 55 of the Constitution (Forty-Second Amendment) Act, 1976. The judgement continues to be a case study for law students and lawyers alike.

This early exposure that Rohinton received fresh out of law college was a tremendous inspiration for him. At Harvard, he majored in US constitutional law, and worked briefly for a year in New York with a law firm specializing in shipping matters. On his return to India, he decided to be on his own and practise independently of his father. 'While my father was in Delhi, I decided to remain in Mumbai. I joined Bomi Zaiwala, who coincidentally used Sir Jamshedji Behramji Kanga's chamber, popularly known as "Chamber No. 1",' Rohinton says.

Rohinton did not receive any stipend or remuneration when he began practising as a junior in Mumbai. What he gained, however, was a solid early experience—a good start, and the reputation of being associated with Chamber 1. In Mumbai, he got the opportunity to argue for theatre artist Vijay Tendulkar and his controversy-marred play *Sakharam Binder*. 'These two cases proved to be the turning points of my life,' Rohinton says with a sparkle in his eyes.

Two other important cases helped him gain invaluable experience at an early age. One against well-known lawyer and Advocate General of Maharashtra H.M. Seervai in the *Needle Industries* case, and the other against former Attorney General Soli Sorabjee in the *Swadeshi Cotton Mills* case. Sorabjee was then the Solicitor General of India, and Rohinton had assisted his father in the case. This gave him a great sense of background and a profound idea of the law.

Relocating to Delhi

It was then time to move on. Rohinton decided to relocate to Delhi. This was a significant time for him as it also saw his marriage, and the birth of his eldest daughter, Nina, in 1986.

Rohinton married Sanaya Contractor on 16 December 1983, and his father gave him his old Fiat car as a wedding gift. Sanaya is an educationist and a teacher trainer. The couple was married in Mumbai, and they shifted to Delhi soon after Nina's birth.

'Not having enough money was something that my wife had to cope with in the first five years of our marriage. Both of us had declined to take any help from our respective fathers,' says Rohinton, remembering those early days of hardship.

M-18 sounds like some secret agency or a military aircraft. But it referred to the address of Rohinton's residence in Green Park in Delhi. During the move, he drove the old Fiat car. 'First, I dropped Sanaya and Nina at the Mumbai airport and then drove up from Mumbai to Delhi with all our household items and cutlery and Nina's toys, which my wife was reluctant to leave behind,' says Rohinton. 'With God's grace, the car somehow reached M-18 Green Park safely. But it stopped working altogether the following morning. I had to tow it to the garage for repairs,' he says.

Rohinton bought his first Maruti 800 in 1987; he had had sleepless nights for almost a month to arrange for the funds to buy it. As usual, he declined all financial assistance offered by his father and father-in-law. To make it up to Sanaya, the least Rohinton could do was make fifty-odd trips to Mount Abu in their first dream car—the Maruti! Later in time, though they bought other cars, Sanaya feels those early trips in their Maruti 800 were the most exciting and exhilarating for them.

My Senior: My Practice

After shifting base, Rohinton joined senior lawyer K.K. Venugopal. He worked with him for about a year and a half and learnt a lot. His whole family refers to Mr Venugopal as 'Guruji'. Venugopal too feels a lot for Rohinton and is extremely proud of his work and accomplishments. Venugopal would often praise Nariman to others, saying that he was very calm and quiet.

In time, Nariman got his first independent case before a Constitutional Bench. Senior counsel and constitutional law expert Anil Diwan was to lead him in the *Bombay Town Planning* case, but for some reason had walked out at the last minute, leaving Rohinton to fend for himself. Rohinton argued for two and a half days. This was the case that earned him great acclaim. Justice Ontethupalli Chinnappa Reddy went around telling the world how good he was. Chief Justice M.N. Venkatachaliah applauded him in his public speeches. It was a great achievement for such a young lawyer to handle cases so effectively and successfully before a Constitution Bench.

Becoming a Senior

There is an interesting background to Rohinton becoming a senior. It was Chief Justice R.S. Pathak who had laid down the norms for designating a senior advocate, which included the consensus of the full court, a minimum age of forty-five years and twenty years' practice.

'I was thirty-six when Justice Venkatachaliah made me a senior lawyer. His belief was that if a Chief Justice thinks that somebody is outstanding, he should designate him as a senior advocate even if he does not fulfil the required norms, provided the full court says yes. So Venkatachaliah institutionalized this rule and made me a senior counsel at the age of thirty-six,' Rohinton says.

Rohinton lost almost all the cases he argued before geniuses like Justices O. Chinnappa Reddy and A.P. Sen. They would listen patiently and encourage him by putting forth meaty questions to him. Rohinton learnt a lot from these confrontations and was appreciated for his arguments. 'The best thing I learnt was how to lose gracefully. This has been a most rewarding lesson in the earlier part of my career,' he says.

Vodafone and Novartis

Vodafone's $2 billion tax matter and Novartis' case (patent protection of its anti-cancer drug Glivec) are two important cases that Rohinton has been associated with. They are important because they have made a difference to our economy and society.

'I won't call them the best or the most representative ones. These are not great cases,' says Rohinton. He believes that the case that actually built his reputation as an astute lawyer was *K.R. Laxmanan v. State of Tamil Nadu* (1996), a landmark judgement. The apex court considered Section 11 of the Madras Gaming Act, 1930, and concluded that horse racing was a game of skill. The Madras Race Club (Acquisition and Transfer of Undertaking) Act, 1986, was struck down by the Supreme Court on the grounds that it was arbitrary. This was despite the fact that the act claimed protection of Article 31C of the Constitution, which meant taking away the fundamental rights (that of the right to engage in the business of horse racing) when giving effect to the policy of the state. Therefore, two important decisions were given: one, that the protection of Article 31C goes, which has never happened, and second, that an act of the state legislature can be struck down on the ground of arbitrariness.

Some of the other important cases that he has been associated with include *Khoday Distilleries Ltd v. The Scotch Whisky Association* (2008). For the first time, the Supreme Court allowed the Khoday group to use the word 'scotch' on its premium whisky brand, Peter Scot. It rejected the liquor body's allegation that the word 'Scot' was deceptively similar to 'Scotch', which led the consumers to believe that the product had a Scottish connection.

In Rohinton's first written judgement (*Mohd Arif @ Ashfaq v. The Registrar, Supreme Court of India*) as part of a five-judge Constitution Bench of the Supreme Court in September 2014, he held that the review of death sentences awarded in the 'rarest of rare' cases will be heard in an open court by a bench of three judges, where the convicts will be allowed to make oral arguments. In a 4:1 majority judgement, he directed that death-row convicts whose death penalty has been reviewed by a bench of less than three judges can move the Supreme Court within a month to reopen their review petitions. The controversy over whether a review of the death penalty should continue to be done in the privacy of the judges' chambers, or transparently in open court, was put to rest by the verdict. Till now, the practice had been that the judges would hear and dismiss review petitions by 'circulation'—in their chambers—rather than in open court.

In another judgement, *Stock Exchange, Bombay v. V.S. Kandalgaonkar*, Rohinton went on to hold that a stock exchange, being a secured creditor, will get priority in the recovery of debts over the income tax dues of a defaulter member, as the former has a first and paramount lien for any sum due to it. Government debts will have precedence only over unsecured creditors as the Income Tax Act, 1961, does not provide for any paramountcy of dues by way of income tax.

Right to Freedom of Speech on the Internet

In a landmark judgement on the right to freedom of speech on the Internet, Rohinton, who wrote the judgement for the Supreme Court bench in March 2015, struck down Section 66A of the Information Technology Act, 2000, a provision that so far had been widely misused by the police to justify the arrests of Internet users for allegedly posting 'offensive' content on social media platforms such as Facebook and Twitter. Stating that the provision was vaguely worded, which allowed for its misuse by the police, Rohinton said the law hit at the root of liberty and freedom of expression. 'The section is unconstitutional also on the ground that it takes within its sweep protected speech, and speech that is innocent in nature, and is liable, therefore, to be used in such a way so as to have a chilling effect on free speech, and would have to be struck down on the ground of overbreadth,' he ruled, while upholding the validity of Section 69B and the 2011 guidelines that allowed the government to block websites if their content had the potential to create communal disturbance, social disorder or affect India's relationship with other countries.

This first-ever verdict in India on the right to freedom of speech on the Internet was hailed by jurists, politicians, activists, students and citizens alike. Former Attorney General Soli Sorabjee, who appeared in the case, said that 'the judgement is well-researched, well-reasoned and erudite in expression'.

As Solicitor General

Rohinton was fifty-five when he was appointed the Solicitor General of India, and he served from July 2011 to February 2013.

Rohinton believes there is always room for improvement and scope for improvising. 'I am not saying I am flawless. There have been occasions when I have reflected on several cases. If I were to reverse or relook at any particular case, then I would certainly prefer to work again on the *Vodafone* case,' he says. Preparing for that mammoth hearing was one of the most stressful ordeals he had ever faced.

As far as his resignation from the hallowed post goes, *'Kahani mein twist'* (meaning, 'a twist in the tale'), is the best way to sum up the unusual events that occurred during this time. It all happened with the Novartis patent case. Rohinton was representing the company before taking over as the Solicitor General, and the then Solicitor General Gopal Subramaniam was representing the government. Post Rohinton's appointment as Solicitor General, Gopal Subramaniam switched positions, much to the anger of the activists who termed the flip-flop a serious case of conflict of interest, although the parties to the litigation obviously had no issues with the switch.

One day, when someone happened to ask Nariman about his experience as Solicitor General, he answered, saying, 'Miserable!' 'You must be joking,' said the gentleman to Rohinton. 'Much to my chagrin, it was difficult to assess whether I was joking,' he says in retrospect.

His resignation after eighteen months had nothing to do with his credentials. Rohinton 'ultimately resigned from the post of Solicitor General on 4 February 2013 because he didn't see eye to eye with the law minister'. There was a lot of speculation and rumours floating around that there was a difference of opinion on certain issues with the then law minister Ashwani Kumar. 'I had very little to do with Kumar. That's all. I think for me, it was the best thing to be able to get out of this,' says Rohinton.

The Practice and Ethics

Rohinton loves the practice of law. It is not a mere money-making business for him but a very noble profession, one to be respected. He values ethics and ethical practice very highly. 'As a lawyer, Rohinton was an inspiration to young aspirants because of his ethos, and the hard work, passion and commitment he put into every brief,' says Abhinav Mukerji, a young lawyer.

Today, Rohinton is happy that there are a large number of young lawyers who are highly ethical. He believes they need to be promoted. 'I think that they are far better than the so-called top lawyers of today. Top lawyers are not top lawyers because they are in the press, please note that. A top lawyer can only be gauged by judges and other lawyers. There is no third person who gauges them. If you ask a judge or another practitioner who is in the courts all the time, all these young people would be top lawyers in their eyes,' he says.

My Approach

Rohinton never had any juniors. 'I never felt the need to have anyone help me out on daily cases. I preferred to do things on my own. I was never selective in my cases, and chose them on a first-come, first-served basis. But yes, I took limited cases as I always wanted to be sure that I reached the court whenever my matter was called,' he says.

People often ask Rohinton about who or what he is inspired by. 'I think my source of inspiration is all the great scriptures, and perhaps all the great music I hear,' he says.

Rohinton has always believed in achieving things on his own, and in his own way. 'I feel it's the greatest obstacle to have a father who is in the profession, especially if he is a renowned jurist. I chose not to join him as a junior. I wanted to come up on my own. I think for me it was a very important thing,' he says.

Strong professional ethics is what he always stands for. 'It's professional ethics that I have always kept at the forefront. This is what these young budding lawyers should strive for. I feel that you should do your work to the best of your ability and have nothing whatsoever to do with clients outside the court. You should not hobnob with neither your clients nor the press,' he says.

With regard to fees, Rohinton says, 'I honestly feel a lawyer should be entitled to charge whatever fee the market can get him. At the same time, the lawyer should voluntarily offer his services too. There was no reason why a poor chap should not get me. If I am convinced that he cannot afford me, then I will appear for him free of charge. I have done many such cases.'

Code of Conduct

Rohinton believes in the presence of a code of conduct for lawyers. According to him lawyers should never get any publicity. 'You should be there on your own merit. Your judgements should speak for you. Also, you should be absolutely straight and open with the bench and with your opponent in court. And lastly, you should, when opposing a young person, take into account his age and then act accordingly,' he says.

Besides being an idealist and a disciplinarian, Rohinton is also known in wider legal circles for his phenomenal memory. 'I must say, reciting gave way to citing. It's to do with the rigorous training in my childhood. Now there are other Parsi priests who are also lawyers and have a fantastic memory. So perhaps there is a correlation. Jamshedji Kanga had a fantastic memory, and so did Seervai. So it's the priesthood, the training as a child and the genetic pool,' he says with a smile.

Advocate Ritin Rai, who worked closely with Nariman during his tenure as the Solicitor General of India recalls, 'It was always a challenge to prepare for conferences because you knew that your preparation had to be complete or you would quickly be found out. Mr Nariman's breadth of legal knowledge and his incredible memory are always spoken about. But it is his command of the facts of each brief he was entrusted with as well as the clarity of his presentation of the case that stand out for me. His sense of his duty to the court as counsel and his work ethic are traits to be emulated.'

Parsi Priest and Lawyer

Even though Rohinton follows Zoroastrianism, he is a strong believer in the value of all religions for the good of humanity. 'I believe in the truth of all great religions. I am both a Parsi priest and a committed Parsi Lawyer,' he says.

According to him, despite the controversy surrounding the disposal of the dead in his community, he believes the best method of disposal of the dead is the natural method. 'When an animal dies, what happens? Nature takes care of it. You can't have dead bodies on the street. So you have to put them together somewhere so that nature takes care of them,' he says.

What makes Rohinton special? It's a combination that is difficult to achieve—of living what he preaches and his impossibly high IQ. Whether he talks of sports, comparative religion, the Vedas, Buddhism, the Upanishads, the Bible, the Baha'i faith or the Bhagavad Gita, he knows as much as the most learned in that particular community.

Hall of Legal Fame

With a firm stride, arms flailing at times, with fervour and with firmness, Rohinton Nariman walks into the Hall of legal fame . . .

He has a thorough grasp of case laws, the foundation of all litigation. An expert in constitutional and civil law, he has appeared as a lawyer in about 500 reported Supreme Court judgements.

He has also been instrumental in setting up the Supreme Court Lawyers' Welfare Trust, which works for the welfare of lawyers. The trust encourages young talent and supports less-privileged members of the Bar. The trust was founded with a generous donation from Rohinton and the late Chief Justice of India J.S. Verma, who was the founder chairman of the body. Several fellowships were instituted by the trust in 2012. Rohinton contributes regularly and generously to the trust. This is the extent of the work that Rohinton has done for the legal fraternity.

Rohinton is also on the governing board of the Gujarat National Law University, Gandhinagar, and was a member of the Mediation and Conciliation Project Committee of the Supreme Court. He also had the privilege of being a member of the Supreme Court of India delegation which visited the Supreme Court of the United States in 2002, where he presented a paper on mediation.

Rohinton is always focused, has an immense drive and sense of purpose coupled with exceedingly high standards of ethics and morality. However, it is his intellect, his fluency of speech and thought, as is evident in the most complex of cases, that make him stand apart from the others.

Life and Music

Rohinton enjoys spending time at his country homes as he finds the environment there conducive to listen to Western classical music and immersing oneself in books. 'Music and books,' he says, 'are my life and blood.'

His memory for music is as prodigious as his exceptional memory for case law. He has an avid interest in history, philosophy, literature and science. He has a great fascination for the mountains, and is very fond of nature trails and walking in the woods.

Rohinton has very frugal habits and no expensive taste. But he does not hesitate to spend freely on books and musical equipment, and boasts of an excellent collection of both. Rohinton listens to music every evening. He likes Western classical especially the music of Beethoven, Mozart, Wagner and Verdi. Music and musical concerts make him travel all the way to London, Vienna and New York every few years.

He likes holidaying, and has never worked during the court holidays. But whether he is on vacation or at home, he walks every day for at least an hour as he is committed to his health. He walks for an hour a day, and during the holidays, he walks for three to four hours in the hills.

Rohinton does not like to socialize, except to spend time with his friends. He enjoys and deeply values his friendships, especially those formed during childhood.

He has a simple philosophy in life. He would like to reach out to people just to explain to them that it is important to be a good human being. 'I think the single-most important aspiration for anybody is that they should be remembered with fondness. You should be remembered as a dead-straight, honest person. Nothing else matters,' says Rohinton.

Rohinton is blessed to have the talented and gentle Sanaya as his wife, and two charming young ladies, Nina and Khursheed as his daughters.

Rohinton has been a very successful person, and the best way to understand his success would be to recall what Arnold Glasgow says, 'Success is simple. Do what's right, the right way, at the right time.'

THE CASE

Enercon (India) Ltd v. Enercon GmbH
Judgement delivered by bench comprising Justices Surinder Singh Nijjar and Fakkir Mohamed Kalifulla on February 14, 2014

CASE DETAILS

In the course of this seven-year-long legal tussle, Enercon GmbH had entered into a joint venture with the Mumbai-based Mehra Group to set up Enercon (India) to manufacture wind turbines. A technology know-how pact was signed on 12 January 1994.

When the technology pact expired in 2004, the foreign partner wanted to enforce an intellectual property licence agreement (IPLA). While the Indian partners moved the Bombay High Court, seeking resumption of supplies which were stopped by the German JV partner in September 2007, the latter wanted to refer the disputes between them to arbitration. Later in March 2008, the foreign company finally invoked arbitration and sought certain declaratory reliefs from the High Court of Justice, Queens Bench Division, Commercial Court, United Kingdom, including the constitution of an arbitral tribunal under the IPLA. This was objected to by the Indian partners in a Daman trial court, claiming that the IPLA was only a draft agreement and not a concluded contract as claimed by the German firm.

The dispute finally reached the apex court after exhausting all remedies before other legal fora in the country, including the Company Law Board and the different high

courts of Delhi, Bombay and Madras, the appellate courts of
Daman, and the English High Court.

The Supreme Court of India then ruled that only
courts in the country had the right to decide on the issue, a
decision which went against the foreign technology partner.
It asked both the companies to arbitrate and also gave the
Indian courts exclusive jurisdiction over the long-standing
dispute. The apex court held that an averment that the
underlying contract containing the arbitration agreement
was not a concluded contract was not sufficient to avoid an
international commercial arbitration, and that the same was
to be left for the arbitrator to decide.

'The intention of the parties is explicit and clear; they
have agreed that the dispute, if any, would be referred to an
arbitrator. To that extent, therefore, the agreement is legal,
lawful, and the offending part as to the finality and restraint
in approaching a court of law can be separated and severed
by using a "blue pencil",' the judges said.

The Supreme Court, relying on the established
jurisprudence in *Bharat Aluminium Company Limited v.
Kaiser Aluminum Technical Service, Inc.* concluded that by
choosing to apply India's Arbitration and Conciliation Act,
1996 (the Indian Arbitration Act), the parties had made a
choice that the seat of arbitration is India.

What weighed heavily in the minds of the judges that
moved them to decide in favour of arbitration in India was
that although the venue of arbitration was London, the seat
of arbitration was India; the substantive law of the contract,
the law governing the arbitration, curial law and patents law
were all according to Indian law; the IPLA was to be acted

upon in India; the enforcement of the award was to be done under Indian law; the joint venture agreement between the parties was to be acted upon in India; and all the relevant assets were in India.

On what the 'seat' of arbitration really means, the Supreme Court held that it would be rare for the law of the arbitration agreement to be different from the law of the seat of arbitration. Accordingly, once the seat was in India, Indian courts would have exclusive supervisory jurisdiction; English courts cannot have concurrent jurisdiction.

The apex court ultimately sided with the seat of the arbitration for resolving any dispute in an appropriate court rather than the venue (at which hearings may be held). 'Venue'—which is not the same as 'seat' of arbitration—is merely a geographical location of the arbitration proceedings chosen on the basis of convenience. However, it is the seat that actually decides the appropriate court which will have exclusive jurisdiction to support the arbitration proceedings. The only exception is when the agreement is completely silent on the seat. In such situations, it's the venue which will emerge as a crucial factor in deciding the appropriate court. The apex court differed from the Bombay High Court's ruling, saying that merely because the venue of arbitration is chosen to be London, that could not lead to the inference that UK courts could be approached by either the Indian or the German entity to seek interim measures during the arbitration proceedings. The Supreme Court held that courts must strictly follow the 'least intervention' policy in the arbitration process and that they must only play a supportive role in encouraging the arbitration proceedings rather than letting them come to a grinding halt. Otherwise, it would lead to utter chaos, confusion and unnecessary complications.

Surely, the jurisdiction of the courts cannot rest upon unsure or insecure foundations. If so, it would flounder with every gust of wind from different directions. Given the connection to India in the entire dispute between the parties, it is difficult to accept that the parties have agreed that the seat would be London and that the venue is only a misnomer. The parties having chosen the Indian Arbitration Act as the law governing the substantive contract, the agreement to arbitrate and the performance of the agreement, and the law governing the conduct of the arbitration, it would, therefore, be vexatious and oppressive if Enercon GmbH was permitted to compel EIL to litigate in England. This would unnecessarily give rise to undesirable consequences.

Impact

The international outlook and the pragmatic approach followed by the Supreme Court indicates that arbitration law in India has finally evolved to meet the demands of effective and expeditious dispute-resolution mechanisms.

Today, arbitration is being flaunted as a cheap and fast alternative to resolve intricate commercial disputes. However, much time is lost in agreeing to where the actual arbitration will take place. Though arbitration clauses generally leave no ambiguity, clarity on the most important things like seat and venue seem to get buried in bulky commercial contracts.

This landmark judgement is a step in the right direction to bring Indian arbitration law in line with international jurisprudence, and it will aid India in being perceived as an arbitration-friendly jurisdiction.

The judgement, while dealing with faulty arbitration clauses having two different places as seat and venue, has made it amply clear that the selection of the seat of arbitration not only determines the law governing the arbitration procedure but also the rights relating to enforcement of the arbitration awards. This ruling has laid to rest any such ambiguities arising in future cross-border disputes.

On determining whether an arbitration clause is unworkable or incapable of being performed, the judgement stated: 'The courts have to adopt a pragmatic approach and not a pedantic or technical approach while interpreting or construing an arbitration agreement or arbitration clause. Therefore, when faced with a seemingly unworkable arbitration clause, it would be the duty of the court to make the same workable within the permissible limits of the law, without stretching it beyond the boundaries of recognition. In other words, a common-sense approach has to be adopted to give effect to the intention of the parties to arbitrate. In such a case, the court ought to adopt the attitude of a reasonable business person, having business common sense as well as being equipped with the knowledge that may be peculiar to the business venture. The arbitration clause cannot be construed with a purely legalistic mindset, as if one is construing a provision in a statute.'

In other words, if the clause indicates a clear intention to arbitrate, no party can be allowed to take advantage of inartistic drafting of the arbitration clause in any agreement.

It is a well-recognized principle of arbitration jurisprudence in almost all jurisdictions, especially those following the UNCITRAL Model Law, that the courts play a supportive role in encouraging the arbitration to proceed, rather than letting it come to a grinding halt. Another equally important principle recognized in almost all jurisdictions is that of least intervention by the courts.

Winning Arguments

Senior counsel Rohinton Nariman, who appeared on behalf of the Indian partners, argued that for the purposes of fixing the seat of arbitration, the court would have to determine the territory that will have the closest and most intimate connection with the arbitration. He pointed out that in the present case, the provisions of the Indian Arbitration Act are to apply; the substantive law of the contract, the law governing the arbitration and curial law are all Indian law. Furthermore, he argued that the IPLA is to be acted upon in India; the enforcement of the award is to be done under Indian law; the joint venture agreement between the parties is to be acted upon in India; and the relevant assets are in India. Therefore, the seat of arbitration would be India.

He contended that the interpretation proposed by the other side that the venue, London, must be construed as the seat is absurd as neither party is British, one being German and the other being Indian. He submits that the respondents have accepted that the choice of law of the underlying agreement is Indian. But if 'venue of arbitration' is to be interpreted as making London the seat of arbitration, it would make the English Act applicable when it is not chosen by the parties, rendering the parties' choice of the Indian Arbitration Act completely nugatory and otiose.

Nariman also submitted that there are even more clear indicators within the arbitration clause which show that the parties intended to be governed only by the Indian Arbitration Act. Defending why London cannot be the seat of the arbitration, according to Nariman, would lead to utter chaos, confusion and unnecessary complications. This would result in absurdity, adding that the court is required to take due notice of the principle of comity of courts; therefore, where more than one forum is available, the court would have to examine as to which is the *forum conveniens.*

According to Nariman, there are very strong indicators to suggest that the parties always understood that the seat of arbitration would be in India, and that London would only be the venue to hold the proceedings of arbitration. Applying the closest and the most intimate connection to arbitration, he said that having chosen all the three applicable laws as Indian laws (as mentioned before), the parties would not have intended to create an exceptionally difficult situation, of extreme complexities, by fixing the seat of arbitration in London.

Nariman stated that businessmen do not intend absurd results. If the seat is in London, then a challenge to the award would also be in London. But the parties having chosen the Indian Arbitration Act, Chapters III, IV, V and VI and Section 11 would be applicable for the appointment of an arbitrator in case the machinery for appointment of arbitrators agreed between the parties breaks down. Therefore, to interpret that London has been designated as the seat would lead to absurd results.

INDEX

A NOTE ON THE TYPE

Garamond comes from the punch-cutter Claude Garamont (also spelled as Garamond, Latinized as garamondus) (c. 1480–1561). It passes off as a blanket name for many oldstyle serif typefaces. Many Garamond typefaces are associated with the work of a later-era punch-cutter named Jean Jannon, or incorporate italic designs created by Robert Granjon.

Released in 1989, Adobe Garamond was designed by Robert Slimbach for Adobe Systems and released in 1989. It is based on the Roman types of Garamond and the Italic types of Robert Granjon.